Belgium and EC Membership Evaluated

EC Membership Evaluated Series
Series Editor: Carl-Christoph Schweitzer, The University of Bonn

The Netherlands and EC Membership Evaluated
ed. Menno Wolters and Peter Coffey

Federal Republic of Germany and EC Membership Evaluated
ed. Carl-Christoph Schweitzer and Detlev Karsten

Ireland and EC Membership Evaluated
ed. Patrick Keatinge

The United Kingdom and EC Membership Evaluated
ed. Simon Bulmer, Stephen George and Andrew Scott

Denmark and EC Membership Evaluated
ed. Lise Lyck

Italy and EC Membership Evaluated
ed. Francesco Francioni

Belgium and EC Membership Evaluated
ed. M.A.G. van Meerhaeghe

Belgium and EC Membership Evaluated

Edited by M.A.G. van Meerhaeghe

Pinter Publishers, London
St. Martin's Press, New York

Pinter Publishers
25 Floral Street, Covent Garden, London, WC2E 9DS, United Kingdom
and **St. Martin's Press**
Scholarly and Reference Division, 175 Fifth Avenue,
New York, NY 10010

First published in 1992

British Library Cataloguing in Publication Data
A CIP catalogue record for this book is available from the British Library

ISBN 0 86187 106 5 (Pinter)
ISBN 0-312-07911-7 (St. Martin's)

Library of Congress Cataloging-in-Publication Data

Belgium and EC membership evaluated / edited by M.A.G. van Meerhaeghe.
p. cm. – (EC membership evaluated series)
Includes index.
ISBN 0-312-07911-7
1. European Economic Community – Belgium. 2. European Economic Community countries – Economic policy. 3. Belgium – Economic policy.
1. Meerhaeghe, Marcel Alfons Gilbert van, 1921– .II. Series
HC241.25.B3B45 1992 91–43785
341.24'22–dc20 CIP

Typeset by Mayhew Typesetting
Printed and bound in Great Britain by Biddles Ltd, Guildford and Kings Lynn

Contents

List of contributors

Filip Abraham has a Ph.D in economics from the University of Michigan, Ann Harbor, USA. He has been Associate Professor in Economics at the Katholieke Universiteit Leuven since 1987. He has published extensively in the area of European Economic Integration and International Trade, and has also participated in several research projects financed by the European Commission.

Roger Blanpain, Dr. jur., M.A. (Columbia), is Professor at the Katholieke Universiteit Leuven.

Alfred Cahen is Belgian ambassador in Paris. He was formerly secretary-general of the Western European Union.

Jean-Pierre De Bandt, Dr. Jur. (Leuven), lic. political science (Leuven), lic. economics (Leuven), Master of Law (Harvard) is a member of the Brussels Bar and a founding and managing partner of De Bandt, Van Hecke, Lagae (Brussels, New York, London). He is President of the Study Centre on Federalism in Brussels and President of the Brussels Philharmonic Society. He is the author of several books and articles.

Hans De Coninck, Dr. jur., lic. econ., Research Department (legal and financial section) Test Achats (consumer association) Brussels. He has published on consumer law, trade practices and tourism and is a founding member of the European Consumer Law Group.

Servaas Deroose is an economist and an administrator of the Commission of the European Communities. The views expressed in this paper are attributable only to the author in his personal capacity.

Philippe de Schoutheete, Dr. jur. is a Permanent Representative of Belgium to the European Community. He was formerly Belgian Ambassador to Madrid and Director General for Political Affairs at the Belgian Foreign Ministry. He is the author of *La Coopération Politique Européenne* (2nd edn. 1986).

Youri Devuyst studied international relations as well as international and European Law at the Vrije Universiteit Brussels and the Johns Hopkins

School of Advanced International Studies in Bologna and Washington, D.C. He is currently Researcher of the Belgian National Fund for Scientific Research at the Vrije Universiteit Brussels. He has written various articles on EC-US relations, U.S. foreign policy, and European integration.

Luc Hens is Professor of Human Ecology at the Vrije Universiteit Brussels and Director of its Human Ecology Department. He is President of the Bond Beter Leefmilieu, an umbrella organization of environmental NGOs in Flanders Northern Belgium. He is a human cytogenetist by training and has written numerous publications in this field and on human ecology.

Michèle Konings, Economist. Center for Economic Studies at the Belgian Ministry of Economic Affairs and Assistant Professor at the Free University of Brussels. Formerly, research assistant at the World Bank, Washington. Communications and publications on economic policy, economic modelling, public finance, international economics and regional economics.

Marc Quintyn, Dr. in Econ. University of Ghent. Formerly at the Belgian National Bank; currently consultant, Central Banking Department, IMF. Is author of several articles on monetary problems.

Bogdan Van doninck is a sociologist, who has carried out research into farmers' organizations in Zimbabwe. He is currently project manager at the Belgian Science Policy Office in Brussels. He is the author of articles on farmers' organizations in Zimbabwe and Belgium, including (with D. Demblon, J. Aertsen et al.): '100 Jaar Boeren' (1990).

M.A.G. van Meerhaeghe, Dr. Econ., lic. pol. science, was professor at the University of Ghent and a special adviser to the Commission of the European Communities. He is now a visiting professor in international economics and European integration. He is the author of several books, including *Economic Theory. A Critic's Companion*, (2nd edn. 1986) and *International Economic Institutions* (6th edn. 1992).

Jef Vuchelen obtained his PH.D. in economics at Free University Brussels and is now Professor there. He is the author of several books and articles on public finance and monetary problems.

Series introduction

This volume is one in a series entitled *European Community Membership Evaluated*. The series examines the gains and losses of European Community (EC) membership for a number of the twelve states.

Over the entire period since the first steps in European integration were taken, with the formation of the European Coal and Steel Community, the impact of membership upon the individual states has been both a matter of importance to, and an issue for evaluation by, the political parties, interest groups, government elites, researchers and, increasingly, the public at large. The renewed dynamism of the EC in the period following the signing of the Single European Act in 1986, and the approach of the completed internal market by the end of 1992, have raised awareness of EC membership to new heights.

It is against this backdrop that the project leading to this series was undertaken. Policy-makers and the European electorate alike require the information to make informed judgements about national gains and losses (or costs and benefits) arising from EC membership.

- How far have the EC's economic policies brought gains?
- Does EC membership impose constraints on the powers of national and regional/local government, or on the legal system?
- What have been the effects of the hitherto somewhat disparate EC activities in the social, cultural and educational policy areas?
- What are the gains and losses of foreign policy co-operation among the member states?
- How pronounced are the specific national interests of the individual member states?

In order to answer questions such as these, each volume brings together a team of specialists from various disciplines. Although the national teams are composed predominantly of academics, the series is aimed at a readership beyond the confines of the education world. Thus each volume seeks to present its findings in a manner accessible to *all* those affected by, or interested in, the EC. Extensive footnoting of academic literature is avoided, although some guidance is offered on the legal bases of EC policies; a bibliography at the end of each study gives guidance on narrower sectoral impact studies and on further reading.

A distinctive feature of the series as a whole is that a common framework has been followed for all studies. This is aimed at facilitating comparison between the national studies. No systematic international comparative study of this kind has been attempted before. Indeed, for some member states there exists no study of the impact of EC membership. The absence of such a series of studies initially seemed rather surprising. However, as the project progressed, the reasons for this became clearer. It is by no means easy to find a common framework acceptable to the academic traditions of all the member states *and* all the policy areas and academic disciplines involved.

The project co-ordinators experienced these tensions in a striking way. Their international 'summit meetings' meant reaching compromises acceptable to all the diverse academic traditions of the countries involved. Then the individual national contributors had to be convinced of the merits of the international compromises. These negotiations brought many insights into precisely the type of problem faced by EC policy-makers themselves. Hence academic perfectionism has been subordinated to some extent to pragmatism and the wish to address a wider readership.

In some countries, for instance the Netherlands, Great Britain and Germany, up to thirty scholars of various disciplines make up the national team. In other countries, such as Ireland, a team numbers less than ten authors. In the latter, *one* author deals with several parts of a subject-group or even with the whole of a subject-group. In either case, however, authors have assured comparability by making cross-references to subsections of policies.

The basic principle of the project has been to assess the gains and losses of EC membership for the individual state, with the hypothetical alternative in mind of that state leaving the EC. This alternative may be deemed to be somewhat simplistic but it is far more manageable than making assumptions about where individual states would be, had they not joined the EC in the first place. Such speculation is virtually impossible scientifically and would undermine efforts to make the findings accessible to a wider readership. The terms 'benefits', 'gains' and 'positive effects', and 'costs', 'losses' and 'negative effects', respectively, are used synonymously.

The activities of the EC, together with the foreign policy co-operation process EPC (European Political Co-operation), are grouped under four broad headings in the project (see Table A) at the end of this Introduction. *Economic policy* covers a range of EC policies: from the internal market to the Common Agricultural Policy but also including environmental policy. *Foreign relations* comprise not only European Political Co-operation but also the EC's external trade policy and security policy. *Social and educational policy* brings together the rather disparate measures taken in a range of areas, some of which are now coming to be regarded as forming the 'social dimension' of the EC. Finally, the subject area *political and legal system* refers not to EC policies but rather to the EC's impact upon the principles and practices of government.

Each of the EC policy headings is assessed following a common approach. The objectives of the EC policy, and the accomplishments thus far, are assessed against the equivalent set of national policy goals and legislation, many of them common to all countries, some of them obviously specific national ones. The idea, then, is to arrive at a 'balance sheet', both at the level of the individual policy area or sector and, at the macro level, for the member state as a whole. Drawing up the individual sectoral balance sheets has to involve a rather flexible approach. The 'mix' of quantitative and qualitative assessments varies according to the subject matter. There can be no quantitative data on how far foreign policy co-operation has brought gains to national foreign policy; figures may be available, however, on the impact of EC trade policy on national trade patterns. In the case of quantitative data it is important to note that very little, if any, primary statistical research was involved in the project. In consequence, quantitative assessments generally present available evidence from previous studies; they follow no consistent methodological approach, while qualitative assessments are often arrived at for the first time. One further point must be made with regard to the common approach of the project: it is clear that the importance of individual EC policy areas varies from one member state to another.

It follows, therefore, that the weighting, and in some cases the categorization, of EC policy areas will vary between the national studies. To assign the same weight to fisheries policy in the British and Luxembourg cases, for instance, would be irrational. Some national policy goals and national interests are related to specific interests of some member countries; for instance, the German question and the problem of Northern Ireland are specific to Germany, Ireland and the United Kingdom respectively.

The whole project has been brought to fruition under the auspices of 'Europe-12 — Research and Action Committee on the EC'. Created in 1986, Europe-12 brings together academics of all disciplines and from all member states, as well as policy-makers and senior politicians. It aims to inform the policy debate through collaborative research and to raise public awareness of the important issues raised by European integration.

As with any such project, a large number of acknowledgements must be made. A number of the participants took on the additional task of horizontal co-ordination, i.e. seeking to ensure consistency of approach across the national studies. For *economic policy* this was undertaken by Detlev Karsten, Bonn, and Peter Coffey, Amsterdam; for *foreign relations* by Carl-Christoph Schweitzer, Bonn, and Rudolf Hrbek, Tübingen; for contributions on *the political and legal system* by Francesco Francioni, Siena, and K. Kellermann, The Hague; finally, for *social and educational policies* by Bernard Henningsen, Munich, and Brigitte Mohr, Bonn. Sadly, Guenther Kloss, a co-ordinator of the British volume, died during the preparation of the series.

Last but by no means least, we are indebted to the Commission of the EC and to those bodies supporting the project: the German foundations, Stifterverband für die Deutsche Wissenschaft, Essen; Bosch GmbH, Stuttgart; Ernst Poensgen-Stiftung, Düsseldorf; as well as the Government of the Saarland and the Federal Ministry for Science and Technology, Bonn. The British and German Studies were made possible by the support of the Anglo-German Foundation for the Study of Industrial Society, London.

Carl-Christoph Schweitzer
Bonn

Table A: Project's categorization of EC policies and structures

I	**Economic policy**	
	Internal market policy	Agricultural policy
	Competition policy	Environmental policy
	Industrial policy	Fiscal/taxation policy
	Technology policy	Monetary policy
	Transport and communications policy	Regional policy
	Energy policy	
II	**Foreign relations**	
	Foreign policy co-operation	Development policy
	Security policy	External trade policy
III	**Political and legal system**	
	Sovereignty	National legal system
	Parliamentary control of the executive	Judicial procedures
	Electoral system	Maintenance of public order
	Political parties	Protection of fundamental rights
	Regional and local government	State organization
	Policy-making process	
IV	**Social, educational and cultural policies**	
	Manpower (employment/unemployment)	Consumer protection
	Movement of labour and migrant workers	Education and training
	Industrial relations	European identity and cultural policies
	Social security and health	
	Equal treatment of men and women	Media policy

Note: This list was a schematic guideline for the project; not every subsection will be dealt with individually and the sequence is purely illustrative.

Europe-12: Action and Research Committee on the EC

Preface

This volume follows the pattern laid down in the series introduction. It considers successively economic policy (Part I), foreign relations (Part II), the political and legal system (Part III) and social and cultural policies (Part IV), but as is stressed in the introduction, 'the importance of individual EC policy areas varies from one member to another'.

Chapter 1 deals with the Treaty's objectives and the implementation of the Treaty. Some economic-policy aspects are examined in relation to the subsidiarity principle. Social policy, dealt with in Part IV, illustrates the non-observance of this principle. Chapter 2 on competition policy is another introductory contribution considering EC philosophy.

The other chapters in Part I deal with the internal market, agricultural policy, environmental policy, budgetary policy and monetary policy. Part II is devoted to external trade and external trade policy, foreign-policy cooperation and security policy, and policy in respect of less-developed countries. Part III considers successively sovereignty and supranationality, democracy and the rule of law, the primacy of Community law and the Belgian federalization process, while Part IV examines labour migration and relations, consumer protection, and national identity and cultural policies.

It is perhaps worth mentioning that in the monetary (one central bank) and foreign-trade fields, Belgium and Luxemburg pursue a common policy.

It is always difficult to produce a collective work. The authors have different views on punctuality and conciseness, and the text will never be as coherent as a text written by the same author, even when overlapping is avoided. Given the different subjects, a common structure cannot be imposed. Furthermore *le style c'est l'homme*. On the other hand, in the fields covered by this book it is impossible to find a Picco della Mirandola, being at the same time – amongst others – a political scientist, a lawyer, an economist, a sociologist and a person with common sense.

My wife has given useful assistance at every stage of this project. I am very grateful to her.

M. A. G. van Meerhaeghe
April 1992

PART I: ECONOMIC POLICY

Chapter 1

The European Community and the market economy – an introduction*

M.A.G. van Meerhaeghe

In the first part of this chapter we consider the objectives of the Treaty and examine to what extent they accord with a market economy. In the second part we ascertain how far the corresponding precepts of the Treaty have been observed. Finally we deduce some conclusions from both parts.

The objectives of the Treaty of Rome

According to its preamble, the main aim of the Treaty of Rome is 'an ever closer union among the peoples of Europe'. But an 'ever closer union . . . clearly covers a multitude of structures and modalities changing over time and cannot thus . . . partake of a single authentic meaning'. It suggests a 'process on the move' but 'if a process is to go on for "ever" there is an implicit affirmation of a "never"' (Bieber et al. 1985: 8).

The more detailed objectives of the Treaty – as stipulated in Article 2 – are very general: to promote throughout the European Community (EC):

1 a harmonious development of economic activities;
2 a continuous and balanced expansion;
3 an increase in stability;
4 an accelerated raising of the standard of living; and
5 closer relations between the States belonging to it.

One wonders whether there is a difference between the first and the second objective; whether these two aims are not incompatible with the third objective (which does not specify the field to which the stability refers); and whether the fourth aim is not a logical result of the second.

The preamble to the Treaty of Rome underlines the necessity to 'preserve and strengthen peace and liberty'. The Single Act goes further: its preamble refers to the 'principles of democracy and compliance with the law and with human rights' and more particularly to 'freedom, equality and social justice'.

Of course, EC citizens are equal before the law, but – like the member states – they are in fact unequal. The statement by the European Commission that 'the principle of equality means that no state has precedence over another' does not prevent the Treaty from weighting the votes of members.

Hereafter, we will pass in review the economic objectives only of the Treaty and their implementation.

The economic objectives

The political and social objective of 'an ever closer union among the peoples of Europe' is to be achieved by economic integration, as is evidenced by the rest of the preamble and by Article 2: by 'establishing a common market and progressively approximating the economic policies of Member States'. Functional theory seems to have influenced the Treaty: political integration will be the result of economic integration.

Unfortunately, the Treaty contains no definition of a common market. A common market, however, is not an instrument of the integration process, but the ultimate result of the process.

The above-mentioned approximation of the economic policies of member states does not provide any indications as to the kind of economic system the Treaty prefers. Economic systems relate to the organization of economic activity. The decisions of the various economic units may be coordinated either by a central organization or by prices.

In the EC Treaty, Article 3 gives more details about the instruments to be used in order to achieve the common market ('in accordance with the timetable' set out in the Treaty):

- a the elimination, as between Member States, of customs duties and of quantitative restrictions on the import and export of goods, and of all other measures having equivalent effect;
- b the establishment of a common customs tariff and of a common commercial policy towards third countries;
- c the abolition, as between Member States, of obstacles to freedom of movement for persons, services and capital;
- d the adoption of a common policy in the sphere of agriculture;
- e the adoption of a common policy in the sphere of transport;
- f the institution of a system ensuring that competition in the common market is not distorted;

- g the application of procedures by which the economic policies of Member States can be coordinated and disequilibria in their balances of payments remedied;
- h the approximation of the laws of Member States to the extent required for the proper functioning of the common market;
- i the creation of a European Social Fund in order to improve employment opportunities for workers and to contribute to the raising of their standard of living;
- j the establishment of a European Investment Bank to facilitate the economic expansion of the Community by opening up fresh resources; and
- k the association of the overseas countries and territories in order to increase trade and to promote jointly economic and social development.

Finally (and according to the preamble), member states should 'strengthen the unity of their economies and . . . ensure their harmonious development by reducing the differences existing between the various regions and the backwardness of the less-favoured regions'.

'Unity', however, does not imply equality of economic and social conditions in the regions, and intervention in the allocation of resources to the various regions will only distort the working of the market system.

The measures mentioned in (a), (b) and (c) relate respectively to a free-trade area, a tariff union and an economic union. In order to achieve an economic union the coordination of economic policies is also required. This is found in (g) and (h). In some fields the Treaty prescribes not coordination of policies, but a common policy. This is the case in the spheres of external trade relations (b), agriculture (d) and transport (e). These 'mandated' common policies were among the least successful.

A preference for a market economy is revealed in (f). Since this refers to the 'common market' it applies to all fields of economic activity. Contrary to the market principles, however, are (i) and (j). Moreover, (k) results in discrimination, again not in accord with free-trade ideas. The fact is that it was a political *sine qua non*, imposed by France during the negotiations preceding the signature of the Treaty, in order to alleviate the burden resulting from its colonies.

Actually the Treaty was a compromise and the countries in favour of market principles had to accept some 'interventionist' stipulations. Even then, there were opposing groups in each country (e.g. industry and agriculture, employers and unions).

The competition principle has a predominant influence on the Treaty. The founding fathers were inspired by the American 'common market' and US competition policy.

Besides the negatively worded Article 3(f) and the passage in the preamble calling for 'fair competition', there are the celebrated Articles 85 and 86, prohibiting restrictive agreements and the abuse of dominant positions, and Article 90, concerning public undertakings and undertakings to which member countries grant special or exclusive rights. Furthermore, Article 29(b) – relating to the setting-up of the common customs tariff – stipulates that the European Commission must take account of 'developments in conditions of competition within the Community in so far as they lead to an improvement in the competitive capacity of undertakings'. Finally, Articles 92 to 94 relate to state aid distorting or threatening to distort competition and incompatible with the common market.

The Single Act

The Single Act, which entered into force on 1 July 1987, does not detract from the free-trade principles of the Treaty of Rome. It brings under a legal roof the existing political cooperation, the European Monetary System, the environmental policy and the research and development policy. It gives more say to the European Parliament and introduces majority voting in a limited number of fields (not in respect of taxes). Majority voting was thought to be necessary in order to attain the objectives of the White Paper *Completing the internal market* of 1985 (confirmed in the Single Act): the realization of the internal market by the end of 1992.

A broader objective (for 1972) is to be found in the Rome Treaty (a common market: Article 8). In other words, in this respect the Single Act is a step backward, since the internal market should already have been realized (in 1970).

The internal market shall comprise an area without internal frontiers in which the free movement of goods, persons, services and capital is ensured in accordance with the provisions of the Treaty (Article 8a). The difference between the internal market (aim of the Single Act), the common market (referred to in the EC Treaty, *inter alia* in Article 3f) and the economic and monetary union is not clear. We should not forget that the Single Act was drafted in less than six months and contains many ambiguities.

The Single Act contains escape clauses, although they are incompatible with its purpose. A member country may, for example, apply 'national provisions on grounds of major needs referred to in Article 36, or relating to protection of the environment or the working environment' (Article 100 4a). Some articles (Article 8c) are inspired by a two-speed Europe.

The Act is followed by 20 restrictive declarations (no part of the Single Act). One of them raises doubts about the seriousness of the Single Act: 'Setting the date of 31 December 1992 does not create an automatic legal effect' (Declaration on Article 8). In other words, the date is no more than political wishful thinking.

The Single Act refers to the transformation of member states' relations 'into a European Union', a concept introduced in 1974, but omits, once again, to give a definition. The term is 'delightfully ambiguous' (Bieber et al. 1985: 7).

The (Maastricht) Treaty establishing the European Union refers once again to the subsidiarity principle, yet introduces Articles on education and culture.

The subsidiarity principle

Although not mentioned in the Treaty nor in the Single Act, 'subsidiarity' is used more and more in respect of the Community to denote that decisions should not be taken at a higher level if they can be taken at a lower level. In other words, the Commission should not do things that member states can do better. The level (town, province, state) at which a function can be efficiently performed is the right level of government. In fact, the subsidiarity principle is implied in the anti-interventionist philosophy of the Treaty of Rome.

The Report on economic and monetary union in the European Community (Delors Committee) refers to the principle of subsidiarity as follows:

> An essential element in defining the appropriate balance of power within the Community would be adherence to the 'principle of subsidiarity', according to which the functions of higher levels of government should be as limited as possible and should be subsidiary to those of lower levels. Thus, the attribution of competences to the Community would have to be confined specifically to those areas in which collective decision-making was necessary. All policy functions which could be carried out at national (and regional and local) levels without adverse repercussions on the cohesion and functioning of the economic and monetary union would remain within the competence of the member countries.

Nevertheless, the same document mentions several forms of Community economic policy (e.g. regional policy) which can better be left to member states. A definition is still lacking in the Maastricht Treaty (1992) but the Treaty is more explicit with respect of the preferred economic system. Several articles (3A, 102A, 105) emphasize that economic policy should be pursued 'in accordance with the principle of an open market economy with free competition'. This is the case in many other EC documents, 'prompting cynics to suggest that the Commission uses it most readily when trying to increase its power' (*The Economist* 1989: 32). 'Subsidiarity' is 'all the rage among Brussels bureaucrats; the more their actions flaunt the principle, the more frequently they seem to declare themselves in favour of it' (Kellaway 1989).

According to E. Noel, former secretary-general of the Commission, 'Community legislation will become increasingly differentiated. Differentiation is the key to progress in the Community' (*Bulletin of the European*

Communities 1987: 8). His statement seems to prove that too many national competences have been attributed to the Commission.

We shall now examine the extent to which the 'strong free-market disposition' (Emerson 1982: 122) of the Treaty has been respected.

The implementation of the Treaty

The Community established the common customs tariff and eliminated customs duties between member countries 18 months ahead of schedule. Although tariffs and quotas had to be removed, they have been reintroduced in agriculture. The monetary compensatory amounts are in fact subsidies or import taxes (in Germany and The Netherlands where farm prices are approximately 6.5 per cent above the EEC average) and border tariffs (in the other EC countries, with the exception of Belgium, where prices are about 4 per cent below the Community level. Other quotas still exist in the textile sector (the Multi-Fibre Arrangement) and in road haulage (bilateral quotas). In many service sectors (e.g. insurance) progress is slow.

Many technical barriers (e.g. different requirements in respect of safety for electrical appliances) – whose removal necessitates the harmonization of legislation – are sometimes more effective than quantitative restrictions. For the Western European market, Philips has to make 15 types of mixer and 12 types of iron. Production costs are seven to ten per cent higher than they need to be because of the differing requirements of the national markets. The same difficulties apply to numerous other sectors, such as telecommunications.

All this notwithstanding the Court ruling of 1974:

> all trading rules enacted by member states which are capable of hindering, directly or indirectly, actually or potentially, intra-Community trade are to be considered as measures having an effect equivalent to quantitative restrictions.

Among the later, more precise findings of the Court:

> the authorities of the importing State are . . . not entitled unnecessarily to require technical or chemical analyses or laboratory tests when the same analyses or tests have already been carried out in another member state and their results are available to those authorities or may at their request be placed at their disposal. (1981)

The Council adopted a new approach to technical harmonization and standards on 7 May 1985. This approach is based on the mutual recognition of the national tests and certification. Harmonization of legislation is confined to the adoption of the essential safety requirements (or other requirements in the general interest) to which products must conform in order to enjoy freedom of movement throughout the Community. The task of drawing up the technical specifications needed to ensure the manufacture and marketing of products that conform to the essential requirements is entrusted to industrial standardization organizations. However, the harmonization is beset by long delays.

Interventionist bias

The anti-interventionist philosophy of the Treaty has not always been respected. Moreover, it took a long time before the Commission abandoned its monolithic conception of the integration process in favour of a more federalist concept respecting the subsidiarity principle. Hence the belief that movement in this decentralizing direction is necessary if the 1992 target (completion of the internal market) is to be met. P.H. Spaak feared that Europe would lose its coherence by the extension of the Community's activities (Poorterman 1987: 3).

As Victoria Curzon-Price puts it: 'Any student of bureaucracy would expect the Commission to seize every opportunity to expand its range of activities and strengthen its control over Community-related public policies, and he would not be disappointed' (1982: 5). So the Commission is writing papers and setting up committees on all possible aspects of general policy.

The subsidiarity principle and economic policy

In several economic-policy fields the Community disregards the subsidiarity principle. Hereafter we pass some of them in review.

Industrial policy Is there any reason why the Community (or member states) should pursue an industrial policy? According to the Commission it should help in restructuring 'problem sectors'. The Commission proposed conversion measures in declining industries (e.g. in the Colonna Report 1970), but the member states did not respond to it. Later, in the textile and shipbuilding sectors, the common restructuring efforts were not successful. In the textile sector it restricted imports (the Multi-Fibre Arrangement).

In fact, there has been no systematic common industrial policy, except – to a certain extent – in the steel sector. It was based on the provisions of the ECSC Treaty. In this sector it restricted production, to the detriment of the most efficient producers. The steel cartel it created was in contradiction to the objectives of EC competition policy. The Community 'action' in the textile industry and naval construction has not been very successful.

Subsidies and other instruments of industrial policy influence relative prices and consequently the allocation of resources. Distortions also occur as a result of differing price-control systems in some member countries.

The Commission can help industry by creating the common market and by combating subsidies, not by tolerating or even authorizing them. In its 1985 White Paper the Commission deplores that large amounts of public funds are spent 'on state aids to uncompetitive industries and enterprises' (p. 39), but the Commission also wants the 'available resources' to be directed 'away from non-viable activities towards competitive and job-creating industries of the future' (p. 40). However, member states and Community resources have *not* to be directed to whatever industries. This is a task for the private sector which will be guided by the market. Neither the states, nor the Commission, know better than business which are 'the industries of the future'. They lack the information necessary to determine which industries or firms (and regions) will prosper and which will not. It is not surprising that the results of the industrial policies of Western countries have been disappointing.

The 'industrial policy proposed by the Commission cannot be the goal to which Europe aspires' (Mestmäcker 1982: 137). In market economies, restructuring problems should not be solved by the creation of crisis cartels (leading to permanent distortions), but should be left to the price mechanism. Industrial policy in a market economy removes needless restrictions and promotes competition (e.g. by combating restrictive practices and by pursuing a free-trade policy). Industrial assistance may be justified if an economically well-founded activity is impossible because foreign companies receive government assistance, for example, in research and development.

Members' industrial policies fare no better. The assessment of Belgium's industrial policy by the Belgian planning office leads to the conclusion that its efficiency is 'relatively weak' (Gilot 1989: 29). The Organization for Economic Cooperation and Development (OECD) is also sceptical: 'it is not clear that industrial policy has been effective . . . government intervention seems rather to have served to support declining sectors and to make good the operating deficits of public enterprises (1986: 32).

No more than the OECD, the EC managed to develop a common energy policy. Its resolutions and directives had, in fact, no influence on the policies of the member states.

Regional policy In this field the subsidiarity principle is just as little respected. Although there is no mention of regional policy in the Treaty, a Regional Fund was created in 1975 and regional policy is referred to in the Single Act.

Neither national nor Community efforts have led to a decrease of regional welfare differences. These regional policies are generally based on criteria that are changed according to the 'needs'. As could be expected, none of the assisted member states is satisfied with Community assistance.

> This is a major reason why 'regional development policies', which have existed under one or another name for over a century, have tended to fail consistently to remedy regional poverty; by attempting to resuscitate industries declining in response to economic pressures they both doom themselves to failure and guarantee the preservation of a next generation of poor people who will have a legitimate claim for public help.
>
> (Johnson 1973: 227)

Even the OECD is sceptical: 'how far deliberate regional policy measures really can help to reduce disparities is still an open question, especially in countries whose regions are equiped with their fair share of infra-structures' (1987: 7); and:

> apart from areas with particularly severe problems, the efficiency of subsidies to fund some proportion of manpower cost is often disputed. Sometimes they are even set to have perverse effects. The destination of the subsidy is not always known, employees may demand higher nominal wages, the subsidy may also be used to inflate the profits of the aided firm, and it is not always certain that subsidies do have any effect on the employment level.
>
> (ibid.: 14)

The main instruments of Community regional policy are the so-called structural funds (Regional and Social funds, European Investment Bank). In order to correct the way the benefits and the burdens of member countries are spread, the Commission favours this non-agricultural spending, but credits from the structural funds do not necessarily flow where they could be most useful. Moreover, this method does not contribute to Community budgetary discipline.

Offsetting EC budget imbalances (and avoiding excessive net benefits or contributions) for the member states is more transparent than more non-agricultural spending. The 'tolerated' net benefits may tackle 'inequity' and 'regional problems' just as well as bigger budgets, although the Community was never expected to become a redistribution machinery (Schmidhuber 1986: 3).

The European Court of Auditors has doubts about the efficiency of the Community funds for regional policy. Regional aid is not very transparent (the lack of transparency is characteristic for all structural funds) and is often used for non-economic projects. However, a budget safeguard mechanism is unlikely to be adopted. Experience in Commission, Council and Parliament proves that an increase of the Community budget is part of the system. Nobody is concerned about the taxpayer (Willgerodt 1987: 52).

The absence of a safeguard mechanism leads precisely to unexpected transfers: whereas Belgium's, Germany's and the United Kingdom's net contributions in 1989 amounted to 0.49 per cent, 0.44 per cent and 0.29 per cent of GDP respectively (France: 0.07 per cent and Luxemburg 0.88 per cent), the other Member States were net receivers: Ireland: 4.23 per cent, Portugal: 1.15 per cent, Spain: 0.15 per cent, but also Denmark: 0.44 per cent and the Netherlands: 0.26 per cent (Italy: 0.09 per cent), (Gijsen and Haack 1991: 1235). If the Community wants to do something for specific countries, this can be done by increasing their net receipts. Moreover, the Community must intervene when national measures cause distortions.

Community regional aid for Belgium has always been small. In 1975–88 the average yearly amount given, for example, to the Flemish region was 267 million Belgian francs (mainly for the reconversion of regions suffering industrial decline). The new approach after 1988 (programmes instead of projects) did not give rise to a new attitude towards Belgium. Of the structural funds' financial commitments for 1990, Belgium received only 1.4 per cent, representing about 6.5 billion Belgian francs. This small amount – compared to Belgium's GDP and fixed capital formation – may have had some influence on employment, but its overall influence has been negligible. No information is available on that influence. Even if Belgium left the Community it would be no problem to finance this amount, especially since Belgium is a net contributor to the Community. Belgium received, for example, Community aid for a modernization project of water works of Malmédy, a town of 10,000 inhabitants, and for the lay-out of a golf course near the same town. Can Belgium not provide the necessary funds? Does it need the Community for that purpose? What about the subsidiarity principle?

The Community regional policy has little impact on Belgian regional policy. Since the Community policy favours the poorer countries, its drawbacks exceed its benefits in Belgium.

Conclusion

The competition principle has a predominant influence on the EC Treaty (see also Chapter 2). Yet the strong anti-interventionist philosophy of the Treaty has not been respected, even if the Commission occasionally stresses the necessity to 'reinforce the market structure of the European economy' (*An enterprise policy for the Community* 1988: 440). Gaston Thorn, former Commission president, even fears 'that both the president of the Commission and the president of France, entirely supported and followed by Spain's prime minister . . . are pursuing an essentially Socialist path'; and he asks: 'if we are not trying to bring in a dose of Socialism under cover of Europeanization'. A Belgian socialist minister calls the EC 'a dirigiste undertaking'.

The subsidiarity principle is largely ignored (as in the member states), for example in the field of regional and social policies. The competition policy is an example of a dogmatic approach, based on purely legalistic notions (see Chapter 2). Under the motto 'harmonization' the Community would like administrative action to establish the same rules for all member states. A better way of achieving integration is to give competition the task of coordinating the market. The relative success of Germany and Italy in many industrial sectors is due to less government intervention and wider application of market principles.

No more as national states, the Community possesses a knowledge superior to that of its citizens. It cannot be the supreme judge and redistributor' (di Robilant 1987: 26—7). The EC's distribution policy, for example, has given rise to strange results (see above).

The lesson to be drawn from the implementation of the EC Treaty is that the best 'constitutions' are worthless if its provisions are not carried out. It is preferable to have no written constitution rather than a written constitution full of high-flown principles which are not respected.

References

* This chapter is based on part of an article by the author ('The awkward difference between philosophy and reality', *European Affairs*, 1989, No. 1).

Bieber R., Jacqué J. P. and Weiler J. H. H. (1985) 'Introduction', in *An ever closer union: A critical analysis of the Draft Treaty establishing the European Union* (ed.) Bieber R., Jacqué, J. P. and Weiler J. H. H., Commission of the European Communities, Brussels, Luxemburg.

Commission of the European Communities (1987), 'Retirement of Mr Emile Noel, the Commission's Secretary-general', *Bulletin of the European Communities*, September.

Commission of the European Communities (1988), 'Communication from the Commission', *An enterprise policy for the Community* Com 88 241/2 final, 10 May.

Curzon-Price V. (1982), 'The European Community, friend or foe of the market economy?' in *For a free society in the coming decade*, Papers, Mont Pélerin Society, General meeting, Berlin 5—10 September.

'Dictionary time' (1989), *The Economist* 9 December.

Emerson A. M. (1982), 'Comment', *Journal of Common Market Studies*, September—December.

Gilot, A. (1989), 'L'évaluation des politiques industrielles (Un état de la question)', Bureau du Plan, Direction sectorielle, *Planning Papers*, May.

Johnson, H. G. (1973), *The theory of income distribution*, Gray-Mills, London.

Kellaway (1989), 'Eurospeak even leaves the Brussels bureaucrats tongue-tied', *Financial Times*, 30 December.

Mestmäcker, E. J. (1982), 'Competition policy in an industrial society (1973)', in *Standard texts on the social market economy*, G. Fisher, Stuttgart, New York.

OECD, *Belgium Luxemburg* (1986), OECD Economic Surveys, Paris, August.

OECD, *Recent regional policy developments in OECD countries* (1987), Paris.

Poorterman, J. (1987), 'Een zeker besef van grootsheid', *Europabericht*, March.

di Robilant, E. (1987), 'Esigenze etiche e operative della società tecnologica avanzata', in *Libertà e società tecnologica avanzata* (ed.) E. di Robilant, Cidas, Longanesi, Milano.

Schmidhuber, Peter M. (1986), 'Die Europäische Gemeinschaft darf nicht zu einer Umverteilungsmaschine werden', *EG Magazin*, 15 December.

Thorn, Gaston (1989), 'Political issues could hinder integration', *International Herald Tribune*, 25 September.

UNICE (1987), 'La politique de concurrence de la Communauté et les exigences de la compétitivité des entreprises européennes', 24 November.

Willgerodt, Hans (1987), *Weltwirtschaft ohne Marktwirtschaft*, Schweizerischer Handels- und Industrie-Verein, December No. 49.

Chapter 2

Competition policy

M.A.G. van Meerhaeghe

Abuse of economic power in Belgium was governed by the law of 27 May 1960 (loi sur la protection contre l'abus de puissance économique). Since then two draft bills (avant-projets de loi) on competition policy have been drawn up (in 1976 and in 1981), generally founded on the Community's legislation. A bill was deposited in 1986 at the Senate, but owing to the dissolution of Parliament in 1987 it lost its validity. Another bill was deposited at the House of Representatives on 10 September 1990 (projet de loi sur la protection de la concurrence économique). It became a law on 5 August 1991 and will come into force on 1 April 1993.

Hereafter, we assume the main characteristics of EC legislation to be known (see Chapter 1) and we examine the differences between this legislation and the Belgian law. Indeed the law refers frequently to the Treaty of Rome and to the Council Regulation on the control of concentration between undertakings (4004/89: 21 December 1989); the law closely follows the Community legislation.

Poor style and lack of definition

The text – sprinkled with tautologies – is badly written, even after many suggestions by the State Council were adopted (strangely enough, some were ignored). The concepts of competition referred to in the Treaty of Rome are not defined. Definition is also lacking in the legislation of numerous countries and in the writings of many economists (a bad example is set by both Adam Smith and Alfred Marshall). In Belgium the many vague provisions and definitions (for example, 'dominant position', 'abuse') have hindered the application of the law of 27 May 1960.

All this should have encouraged the authors of the law to attach more importance to definition. The law contains one article (Article 1, entitled 'Definitions') which defines only three concepts: 'undertaking', 'dominant position' and, 'minister'. The definition of effective competition is lacking here: it is given in the explanatory memorandum. It is no model of clarity; what is the meaning, for example, of 'dans des limites claires et nettement circonscrites' (garantir le droit à l'entreprise individuelle d'exercer ses activités sur le marché de son choix dans des limites . . .)? The minister claims that the use of 'termes assez généraux' is unavoidable and that the undertakings concerned should consult European jurisprudence!

Organization

Belgian law provides for the creation of an administrative jurisdiction, the Competition Council, which decides on restrictive competition practices submitted to it by the Competition Office, part of the Ministry of Economic Affairs. It also has an advisory function, on its own initiative or at the request of the Minister of Economic Affairs.

The Council is made up of 12 members: six (two of whom are the chairman and vice-chairman) are designated from among the members of the judiciary, six are designated for their competence in matters of competition. Does this imply that the members of the judiciary do not have such competence? There are also 12 alternate members, designated on the same basis. Members are appointed for a six-year period by royal decree deliberated in Cabinet.

It is questionable whether a body of 12 part-time members is more efficient than a small number of full-time members. Budgetary difficulties perhaps explain the choice. Italy, with similar problems, rightly chose a collegiate body of five full-time members, the Guarantee Authority. Belgian law does not provide any details about competence. Political interventions have to be feared.

The law institutes an Advisory Commission representing all sides of industry: trade unions, employers, agriculture, trade. Experience with other advisory bodies shows that most of their recommendations consist of as many opinions as there are members. Moreover it is a step in the procedure (cf. Article 28) hindering speedy decisions. We may question the usefulness of this advisory body.

Other deviations and similarities

The relevance of some supplements in the Belgian law to EC legislation may be questioned. These deviations are not explained. Whereas in the Concentration Regulation (recital 15) a market share of the undertakings concerned not exceeding 25 per cent is presumed compatible with the common market, the law lowers this percentage to 20 per cent (Article 11). It could be increased, for example, if too many cases are submitted.

In addition, total minimum turnover for application of the law is fixed at more than one billion francs, while in the Concentration Regulation the aggregate Community-wide turnover of each of at least two of the undertakings concerned must exceed 250 million ECU (Article 1: the aggregate worldwide turnover of undertakings concerned must exceed five billion ECU).

This percentage (20) and this amount (one billion francs) are too small, especially in a country, such as Belgium, largely open to competition. Not even the Commission went below 45 per cent (United Brands), although it does not exclude it (Commission 1981: 112).

In other fields it would be better if the law had not followed the Community example. 'My home is my castle' is certainly not the rule in Belgium. Many pretexts justify the right to search people's home or premises. This law again provides for the possibility of search. In my opinion only serious indications of infringement could justify a search. Guarantees of confidentiality are higher in the United States.

The paperwork in relation to information needed could also be reduced to a great extent. Is it really necessary to provide a list of suppliers and customers for each product group, as is customary in the European Community? Again much less information is required in the United States. But the law is silent in this respect. Does the Ministry and the Council really need 75 days (after a one-month 'reflection' period) in concentration cases to reach a decision? This period may even be extended, e.g. when translation of some documents is necessary. The long period required for a decision may discourage legitimate mergers. A speedier procedure must be possible. For agreements there is no time limit at all.

Competition policy de facto an industrial and social policy?

Article 85,*3* – the text of which is taken up in the law – provides that the provisions of Article 85,*1* may under certain conditions be declared inapplicable in the case of an agreement, decision or concerted practice 'which contributes to improving the production or distribution of goods or to promoting technical or economic progress, while allowing consumers a fair share of the resulting benefit'.

In contrast to the ECSC treaty, the Treaty of Rome contains no provisions on mergers. Nevertheless, the Court of Justice assumes that Article 86 allows control of concentration proposals by an undertaking occupying a dominant position. Because of uncertainty in this field the Council approved on the basis of Articles 87 and 235 of the Treaty the abovementioned Regulation on concentration on 21 December 1989. Article 235 of the Treaty seems to have been used not to pursue 'one of the objectives of the Community and this Treaty' but rather to expand on the Treaty. The Regulation went into force on 21 September 1990. There is reference in Article 2 to 'the interests of the intermediate and ultimate consumers', 'the development of technical and economic progress, provided that it is to consumers' advantage'.

Although the Regulation seems to consider the maintenance of effective competition as the main yardstick in judgements in respect of mergers, the reference to other considerations could be a loophole for the implementation of an industrial policy. In fact, some commissioners in charge of competition have stated that: 'Industrial-policy reasons also justify a merger regulation' (Sutherland 1988).

The director-general for competition, C.D. Ehlermann, believes that the criterion 'market dominating position' will take priority (Wisdorff 1990). But it is a belief which may not necessarily be shared by one of his successors. This weakness could have, but has not, been avoided in the Belgian text. On the contrary, the reference to 'general' terms has been extended. Not only are there references to 'technical and economic progress' (see above), 'to the interests of the intermediate and ultimate consumers' (Article 2), but also to 'public economic interest' (Article 10). What is the meaning of 'public economic interest'? The vagueness of this and other terms adds to the uncertainty of the law for the firms affected. Nobody knows how far 'public interest' considerations will be taken into account. There is a risk that Council decisions will be more influenced by political than economic considerations.

In the list of possible exemptions (Article 2,*3*; cf. Article 85,*3*) are added agreements between small- and medium-sized undertakings reinforcing their competitive position. There is no explanation why deviation from Article 85 is necessary. Why should these undertakings be treated in a different way than bigger companies? Here again there is a real risk of politically motivated decisions. Why trade-union representatives may ask the Council to be heard (Article 27,2) is puzzling. Competition policy is not part of social policy.

While a first requirement of a free-trade economy is the absence of price control, the explanatory memorandum believes that competition policy must be matched by price control — although it admits that more flexibility in this field will be possible! Price control hinders price reductions and favours restrictive agreements.

Price control may be a measure 'having equivalent effect' to quantitative restrictions on imports and as such it is prohibited (Article 30 of the Treaty of Rome). But the Court's jurisprudence has been rather timid in this respect. The explanatory memorandum pretends — and it is not alone in this respect — that 'competition policy is not an objective in itself' ('la politique de concurrence n'est pas une fin en soi'), ignoring the fact that the competition principle had a predominant influence on the Treaty (cf. chapter 1).

National versus Community rules

Concurrent implementation of EC and national competition rules is possible, in as much as it does not prejudice the uniform application of competition rules in the Community. However, national authorities may ban an agreement about which the Commission has declared by letter of comfort that it will not intervene (it is no formal exemption). Equity considerations require that account should be taken of previous sanctions.

In addition to their advisory role, member states can be involved in the Community procedure in respect of concentrations if they fear damage to competition in a 'distinct' market in their national territory. If the Commission agrees, they can consider the concentration under their national law (Article 9 of the Council Regulation). In fact, possible complainants would be better off to proceed before national courts, which can grant damages, whereas the Commission can only impose fines. Moreover, the Commission is to some extent a judge in its own cause. But the costs involved in proceeding before national courts are higher. National courts may also prefer to seek a preliminary ruling from the Court of Justice clarifying how Community law should be interpreted in the case concerned.

Conclusion

Community law is directly applicable in the member states; it is part of national legislation. A national legislation makes sense only if, for example, concentrations refer merely to the Belgian market (or parts of it) *and* do not influence intra-Community trade. Given the Court jurisprudence in this respect, 'national' concentration would be extremely rare, at least in Belgium with a surface of 30,000 sq. km. So we doubt whether a national competition legislation is necessary.

Logically, competition should be matched by free price formation. Hence the absence of provisions repealing price control is striking in Belgian law. This would not exclude government powers in order to take provisional and punctual measures in exceptional circumstances. Since Belgian law is based on Community legislation and policy, its appraisal boils down to an assessment of Community legislation. The Belgian government seems not to have made such an appraisal. Community competition policy has been based on American anti-trust legislation. But in recent years the American belief in this legislation has wavered. Oligopolies and even monopolies are not necessarily dangerous, in as much as freedom of entry is guaranteed. In most oligopolies competition is very strong. Concentration may be compatible with competition. Just because four enterprises account for 80 per cent of production in the detergent sector does not mean that there is no competition. At a time that many academics admit this, the Commission and some member states are increasing their powers to combat concentration.

The Commission has adopted a case-by-case legalistic approach. As the Union of Industries of the European Community puts it: 'Until recently, the Community's competition policy has generally been applied in a dogmatic manner' (Union: 2). Complaints by firms relate to 'the dilatory nature of proceedings' (Bernini 1981: 354) to obscure drafting techniques and to 'formulas . . . that . . . sometimes amount to real grammatical and syntactical acrobatics (ibid.: 355). Simpler rules on the application of competition laws are in any case necessary (*Handelsblatt* 1987).

There is no coherent and logical evolution in Community policy. There is even 'withdrawal from positions that seemed at the time to be well established'. Hence the 'very serious consequences that the resultant uncertainty entails for operators who are forced to make a prior judgment as to whether the practices in which they wish to engage are or are not permissible' (Bernini 1981: 337). The Commission often does not know exactly what it wants. There was a time when it stimulated the creation of large European companies, for example by mergers; later these mergers came to be regarded with much distrust.

The Community's interpretation of, for example, 'relevant market', 'products involved', 'concerted practices' and 'dominant position' has changed in the course of time. The Court and the Commission often consider even firms subject to substantial competition and without the power to determine prices to be dominant; the fact that market shares are high – 45 per cent in the case of United Brands – is not necessarily proof of dominance. In the same case the Commission expressed the opinion that 'charging a price which is excessive because it has no reasonable relation to the economic value of the products supplied is . . . an abuse'. But given the liberal inspiration of the EC Treaty, the 'economic value' should be determined by the market. Moreover, it is quite normal for an undertaking to charge what each market can bear.

Even experts close to the Commission believe that competition policy should 'focus more selectively on the cases of greatest importance to the Community market, with lesser intervention wherever only national or local markets are mainly affected' (*Efficiency, stability and equity* 1987: 82). Some aspects of competition policy raise questions. What dangers may result from exclusive distribution agreements? Small- and medium-sized enterprises in particular have difficulties in finding distributors when parallel imports are allowed. The Commission considers only competition between sole distributors and forgets that competition also exists between different brands.

The Commission sometimes takes into account considerations which have nothing to do with competition policy. For example, the block exemption relating to automobile distribution contains provisions in respect of the prior notice to be given if a dealer is dismissed; this is social policy, not competition policy. National authorities would do better to try to influence Community competition policy than to adopt Community legislation without careful consideration.

References

Bernini, G. (1981) 'The rules of competition', *Thirteen Years of Community Law*, European perspectives, Brussels, Luxemburg, European Communities.

Commission of the European Communities (1981) *Tenth Report on Competition Policy*, Luxemburg, Office for Official Publication of the European Communities.

Efficiency, Stability and Equity: a strategy for the evolution of the economic system in the European Communities, (1987) report of a study group appointed by the Commission of the European Communities and chaired by T. Padoa-Schioppa, Brussels, 10 April.

Handelsblatt (1987) 'Die Deutsche Industrie beklagt die Unverständlichkeit der Brüsseler Texte', 14 September.

Sutherland, P.D. (1988), *EC Competition and Community law*, speech delivered in London, 22 April.

Union des Industries de la Communauté Européenne (1982) *La politique de la concurrence de la Communauté et les exigences de la compétitivité des entreprises européennes*, Brussels, 24 November.

Wisdorff, E. (1990) 'The Brusseler "task force" ist schon voll einsatzbereit', *Handelsblatt*, 20 September.

Chapter 3

Internal market policy

M.A.G. van Meerhaeghe

At first sight it is strange that no cost-benefit analysis of EC policy effects on Belgium in this important field has been made: 'a systematic balance sheet is not available' (Ministry of Foreign Affairs and Development Cooperation: I). Indeed, it is difficult to isolate among the many factors influencing Belgium's economic growth and other macroeconomic components, such as trade and employment, those influenced by European economic integration.

Even without EC integration, the efforts made in Benelux, OEEC, GATT and other international organizations to eliminate trade barriers would have increased the openness of Belgium's economy. Belgium's policy always favoured trade liberalization. Its tariffs were relatively low. Without the EC Belgium's trade and GDP would have progressed, as it had before 1958. The EC provided an additional guarantee to trade stability, but it is impossible to calculate the size of the EC effect. The fact that countries similar to Belgium and not members of the EC (e.g. Switzerland) show better economic performance than Belgium, tends to demonstrate that the EC effect was not important.

Belgium as well as the EC pursue very general goals such as economic growth, price stability, international security and peace. This contributes to a smooth cooperation. It does not exclude divergent opinions on policies tending to realize these goals. Belgium's withdrawal from the EC would not have influenced its objectives.

Here we examine whether EC membership has influenced Belgium's economic structure. First we provide some information on Belgium's economy.

Economic structure

Belgium is a small country (30,500 sq. km.) of 9,9 million people accounting for 3.2 per cent gross domestic product (GDP; at current prices and current purchasing parities) of the EC. Its average GDP slightly exceeds (5 per cent) the average of the Community (1990). Among Belgian assets are its geographic position in the centre of Europe, its qualified work-force, its extensive transport network and its favourable economic and social environment.

In 1921 Belgium and Luxemburg (2,586 sq. km and a population of 374,900) concluded an economic union, the Belgian-Luxemburg Economic Union (BLEU). Whereas the Belgian GDP amounts to 6,180 billion francs, that of Luxemburg equals 278 billion francs or 4.5 per cent of the Belgian GDP. In 1922 Luxemburg adopted the Belgian customs tariff. Belgium concludes the commercial agreements, but after consultation with Luxemburg. Only the steel and bank sectors of the two countries are comparable.

Even if the BLEU is not a complete customs union (excise duties, for example, are not unified) it is more than a customs union since there is only one central bank, the National Bank of Belgium. Payments between the two countries are free and there is a common balance of payments. Trade statistics refer to both countries (Meerhaeghe 1987). The BLEU exports 3.2 per cent and imports 3.1 per cent of world trade and it is the tenth largest exporter and importer. Belgium has an open economy and its openness has increased – as in most other countries – since the end of the Second World War. In 1988 its exports represented 58.7 per cent of GDP, its imports 60.8 per cent (cf. chapter 8). In respect of exports the corresponding figures for the Flemish region, the Walloon region and the Brussels region are respectively 73.8, 21.2 and 5.

The internationalization of the Belgian economy increased with large foreign investments, which started in the 1960s. Many multinational companies have affiliates in Belgium. Among the 50 most important Belgian industrial enterprises, 26 are affiliates of international groups. In the list of the 100 largest European companies there are only two Belgian enterprises, the first of which, Petrofina, is only number 57.

Medium-sized enterprises dominate the Belgian economy. Their size is not necessarily inadequate in view of the common market. The increasing number of mergers and acquisitions of large companies is even alarming, since experience so far in the mergers and acquisitions field has often been unfavourable.

Internationalization also applies to the financial sector. On 15 March 1991, out of a total of 90 banks operating in Belgium, 63 were foreign (37 of which were European). They accounted for half of the sector's assets, one fifth of its deposits, 40 per cent of its outstanding stock of foreign loans and 25 per cent of its stock of domestic loans. In 1987 foreign assets as a share of total assets amounted to 57 per cent, while non-residents' claims on the banks represented 71 per cent of bank liabilities. The Belgian banking sector is one of the world's most internationalized. Other structural characteristics are high 'tertiarization' (see table 3.1) and an important role played by the public authorities, whose total receipts represent nearly half of the GDP.

Table 3.1 *Belgium. Structure of output and performance indicators (in per cent of total). Structure of GDP (1) and share of total investment (2) 1989; share of total employment (3) and productivity growth (4) 1987*

	(1)	(2)	(3)	(4)
A Structure of output and economic performance (constant prices)				
Agriculture, hunting, forestry and fishing	2.1	1.9	2.5	– 5.1
Mining and quarrying	0.3	0.3	0.6	12.3
Manufacturing	23.0	25.9	24.3	3.9
Electricity, gas and water	3.6	3.7	0.9	7.2
Construction	5.8	2.6	5.7	2.5
Tradeable services*	39.7	49.3	20.2	2.4
Non-tradeable services**	17.0	8.8	29.9	0.1
Total market sector	91.5	92.6	84.0	2.1
Non-market sector	12.8	7.4	16.0	1.9

B Other indicators (current prices, 1988)
R & D as per cent of value added in manufacturing sector: 5.0; Total R & D expenditure as per cent of total GDP: 1.8; Government-funded R & D as per cent of total: 28.7; Breakdown of R & D workforce by size of establishment (in persons-years) 0 to 99: 17.3; 100 to 499: 18.7; 500 to 999: 9.1; more than 1,000: 54.9; Workforce: 22,044.

* Wholesale and retail trade, restaurants and hotels, transports, storage and communication, finance, insurance and real-estate affairs.
** Business services, community, social and personal services.

Source: OECD.

Belgium's industrial structure underwent no important changes in the postwar period. Belgium is still a country producing mainly products for which international demand is rather weak, many of them semi-finished products. In fact, this specialization could be favourable for small countries (Drèze 1960).

Belgium's export performance is best in these mature or traditional industries. The sectors concerned include chemical products, glass, cars, carpets, rubber, chocolates, jewels and beer. However, as just mentioned, growth of world demand for these products is slow. Exports to the EC still experience restrictions (chapter 1). Among the protected sectors are industries working mainly for public authorities or enterprises such as the railways and energy production. These enterprises are too numerous in Europe and often work below capacity. Some of them have already merged. Other weak industries experience competition from new industrializing countries, for example, naval construction and electric equipment.

Belgium's handicap is that the decision-centres of many sectors – cars, glass, chocolates – are abroad. One third of the most important companies are in foreign hands: the US accounts for a quarter of the foreign total (in the eighties takeovers originated predominantly with Belgium's neighbours, especially France); they produce nearly half of Belgium's GDP. This implies that legislation in respect of foreign investment is important. Foreign investors want security and do not like regulations being modified too often. Unlike their French counterparts Belgian governments never showed the same concern for important economic decisions to be taken in accordance with Belgian interests.

Rigidities

The Belgian economy is also characterized by many rigidities, especially in the social sector. An easily available unemployment benefit, together with insufficient control and limitless duration, favours high unemployment rates: women are responsible for 40 per cent of unemployment. The substantial duration of unemployment is related to educational qualifications. Other rigidities relate to wages, working hours, recruitment and discharge conditions. The fact 'that there is virtually no time limit on unemployment insurance may have a disincentive effect on labour supply in some cases' (OECD 1988–9: 88). The average participation rates of men and women between the ages of 60 and 64 were 20.3 per cent and 4.1 per cent respectively in 1987, much lower than in Belgium's main partner countries.

Complete and automatic wage indexation contributes to inflationary pressure, especially when large increases in oil prices occur. During the 1970s too large wage-rises led to more capital-intensive investment and a decline in employment. To prevent wage-rises harmful to Belgium's competitive position, an act to safeguard competitiveness (January 1988) has to be observed in collective bargaining. If the government considers that this should not be the case, it will intervene.

It is striking that during the postwar period Belgian governments did not try to eliminate the many rigidities characterizing the economy. This explains the high budget deficit, one of the most important in the EC (6.5 per cent of GDP in 1989). The public debt is equivalent to 128 per cent of GDP (1990) and interest payments represent 11 per cent of GDP and a quarter of current general receipts. As the OECD (1990–1: 95) puts it: 'The adoption of a whole series of structural reforms – pertaining to labour-market policies, the system of direct taxation, the public services, social expenditures and the free play of competition – is vital, not only to allow the bolder actions needed to put the rehabilitation of the public finances on a more rapid and secured path, but also to instil greater efficiency in the economy, thereby enhancing its supply capacity.'

Conclusion

Without the EC the Belgian economy would have progressed, as it did before 1958. The EC effect – which is impossible to measure – is probably very small. Belgium's economic structure did not change very much during the interwar period. Belgium is still producing products the world demand for which is rather weak. It is further characterized by many rigidities, especially in the social sector. This gives rise to a high government deficit, limiting the government's possibilities of stimulating the economy.

References

Belgique cap 92 (s.d.) (1988) Quelques enjeux majeurs, contributions au colloque, Bureau du Plan, Brussels, 12 December.

Belgique cap 92 (s.d.) (1988) Actes du colloque, Bureau du Plan, Brussels, 12 December.

Drèze, Jean (1960) *Quelques réflections sereines sur l'adaptation de l'industrie belge au Marché Commun*, Comptes rendus des travaux de la Société Royale d'Economie Politique de Belgique, December.

National Bank of Belgium (July–August 1987, November 1987, November 1988), 'L'évolution structurelle de l'économie Belge', *Bulletin de la Banque Nationale de Belgique*.

OECD economic surveys, *Belgium Luxembourg, 1988–1989* (1989), Organisation for Economic Cooperation and Development, Paris.

OECD economic surveys, *Belgium Luxembourg, 1990–1991* (1990), Organisation for Economic Cooperation and Development, Paris.

Meerhaeghe, M.A.G. van (1987) *The Belgium-Luxemburg Economic Union*, Tilburg, SUERF.

Ministry of Foreign Affairs and Development Cooperation, Directorate-General for foreign economic relations (s.d. 1988), 'Study on the influence of 1992 on intra-Community trade of the BLEU'.

Chapter 4

Agricultural policy

Bogdan Van doninck

At the end of the Second World War, Belgian agriculture had several features that are still characteristic of agriculture in some Southern European countries: an agriculture with relatively low productivity, practised by a large number of farmers on small farms. This was the result of an agricultural policy that had been followed in Belgium since the great agricultural crisis at the end of the last century: a protectionist policy, favouring an agriculture based on the family farm. Safeguarding the national food supply as well as protecting rural life-space were both important arguments used by the architects of this policy. Belgium, one of the earliest and most industrialized countries, thus kept a protected and relatively backward agriculture.

Background

It is impossible to answer the hypothetical question: 'What would Belgian agriculture have been like had there been no common agricultural policy?' The European integration caused both qualitative and quantitative changes in Belgian agriculture, some of which will be described later. The most important change, however, concerns the way Belgian agriculture is integrated in society at large. Before the European integration, agriculture in Belgium was only partly seen as an element of the national economy. Agriculture was not only valued for its contribution to the economy, but also as an element which permitted the survival of the rural world. European integration meant a radical change. Agriculture, although the subject of some special measures, came to be seen as just another form of economic activity: a supplier of inputs to the agro-industry and a buyer of capital goods and intermediate products. The social element was still taken into consideration, but only in the sense that structural changes had to be accompanied by social measures in order to alleviate possible negative consequences. The protection of rural life in itself was no longer sufficient justification for the protection of an outdated agriculture. To put it bluntly: before European integration, agricultural policy was to a large extent a social policy with economic features; after European integration it was an economic policy, accompanied by social measures.

For Belgian agriculture, European unification meant exposure to competition from countries which had a more efficient agricultural system. To this challenge of European unification two answers were possible: the reinforcement of protectionist measures or a policy of adaptation in order to survive in a competitive environment. Belgium chose a guided adaptation of agricultural structures, which in the long run has led to deep changes. The contribution of agriculture to the GNP was only +/- two per cent in 1989: 115.8 thousand million francs out of a total of 5,656.5 thousand million. However, we are talking here about a specialized and productive agriculture. In the European context, Belgian agriculture represents roughly one per cent of the agricultural acreage, one per cent of the agricultural population but three per cent of the value of agricultural products. Thus, in terms of product value, its performance is above the average attained by European agriculture.

In the framework of European integration, a special agricultural policy was designed. First of all, the Second World War still fresh in people's memories, came the economic and strategic need for food self-sufficiency. Furthermore, it was necessary to promote structural changes – increase of scale, mechanization, the intensification of production, regional specialization – and an increase in productivity, which would drain off the excess labour force into other branches of the economy.

The common agricultural policy unfolded in several stages. The first period saw a general support of increased production. Later on came a more selective policy, aimed at modernizing viable enterprises and eliminating marginal ones. Subsequently, when scarcity was generally replaced by growing agricultural surpluses, a more restrictive policy was followed, laying more responsibility on the producers. Recently, product quality, consumer protection and care of the environment have been given more attention, and serious thought paid to changing the common agricultural policy fundamentally. Direct support to incomes is one component of a possible new policy.

Changes at national level

Policy-making

In Flanders particularly, farmers organized themselves after the agricultural crisis at the end of the nineteenth century, forming the 'Belgische Boerenbond' (literally the 'Belgian Farmers' League'), aimed at protecting agriculture and more generally at defending a rural Catholic world threatened by economic plagues as well as by ideological foes (i.e.

liberalism and socialism). The Boerenbond gradually managed to establish a political and ideological framework for the Flemish rural population and to build a group of agriculture-based companies. To achieve this, it could rely on the Catholic church, on a privileged relationship with the majority political party in Flanders (and in Belgium), and on a network of companies for grouped supply and marketing, cattle-cake plants, insurances, a savings bank, etc. (Demblon et al. 1990). The organization managed to become a privileged partner for the government on the one hand; on the other hand it managed to persuade its members to accept its policy. Other farmers' organizations, including the Walloon ones, were either too weak or unwilling to impose another policy (Mormont and Van doninck 1992).

In Belgium, agricultural policy has seldom been the subject of public political debate: ministers and leaders of the big farmers' organizations have worked out its outline together. This situation is far from unique: the 'social concertation' that has existed for several generations involves representatives of pressure groups in negotiations for preparing certain policies and has made them become directors of specialized parastatal institutions. In agriculture this is more specifically the case for institutions involved in marketing, agricultural credit and research. With European unification, the high degree of technicality of agricultural problems has strengthened this tendency: this gives the impression that decisions are taken at the European level and can merely be implemented in the different member states. In Belgium, the sector that absorbs the greatest part of the European budget is the one which is least subject to public political debate. This should further be seen as an element of Europe's 'democratic deficit'.

The big farmers' organizations have accepted the major lines of the common agricultural policy. It would be important to study how the Boerenbond, the largest farmers' organization, developed from an organization defending the countryside into a professional organization, supporting the most dynamic farmers and owning an important agro-industrial conglomerate. Notwithstanding the resistance of a large proportion of farmers, who would have preferred a continuation of the protectionist policy, Belgian decision-makers (i.e. both the government and the farmers' organizations) have adopted a policy for transforming Belgian agriculture. This transformation has had effect at both national and farm levels.

Concentration

The protectionist policy in Belgium was the traditional cornerstone which defended the prices of agricultural products (even though this led to considerable smuggling, especially with Holland, where agricultural prices were lower). The disappearance of the national protective measures was originally offset by price-support measures. This price support, part of the common agricultural policy, mainly benefited the larger farms (Brown 1990) but still helped some marginal farms to survive: price support initially supplied the 'oxygen' for two out of every ten farms. As price support was gradually withdrawn, farms had to be more profitable in order to survive in a competitive environment. Smaller, marginal farms disappeared.

Support to larger farms and the disappearance of marginal farms led to a concentration of Belgian agriculture. In 1959, there were about 269,000 farms (either as a main or a secondary activity). In 1970, only 184,000 remained. By 1985, the number had decreased to 104,619 (of which 29,949 farmed as a secondary activity) and by 1989 to 89,100. The acreage decreased from 1,540,300 ha. in 1970 to 1,389,900 ha. in 1985. (In 1880, just before the agricultural crisis, the acreage had reached its highest point ever: 1,972,000 ha. or 65 per cent of the territory.) Employment in agriculture decreased proportionally: from 1960 to 1986, the number of labour units decreased from 338,000 to 105,000. (In 1895 the figure was 773,000, out of a total population of 6.7 million.)

The result of this decrease in the number of farms was an increase in the average acreage per farm from 6.2 ha. in 1959 to 8.4 ha. in 1970, 12.5 ha. in 1980 and 15.2 ha. in 1989. The farms to disappear were mainly the smaller, marginal ones (Van Haeperen 1987a). It is expected that in the year 2000 the average Belgian agricultural business will measure 25 ha. and that by that time another 15,000 farms will have disappeared.

The picture, however, is not the same for all sectors. Specialization in more market-oriented sectors appears to offer a better chance of survival: the number of horticultural enterprises decreased from 11,641 in 1959 to 8,127 in 1983. This decrease in numbers was slower than the average decrease: in 1959, horticultural enterprises formed 7.19 per cent of the total, whereas their share of the total number of Belgian exploitations in 1983 had risen to 12.43 per cent.

Increase in yield

This concentration was coupled with an increase in productivity: despite an average yearly drop in the number of labour units (and a slightly decreasing acreage), the average yearly output value rose by 2.7 per cent (at constant prices). This means an average increase in labour productivity of 6 per cent per year.

Table 4.1 gives an overview of the development of the gross product value over the years (in Belgian francs, constant prices, base: 1980).

One result has been increased self-sufficiency. Belgium is self-sufficient for potatoes, well exceeds self-sufficiency for sugar (269 per cent), but reaches only 50 per cent for cereals. For vegetables the degree of self-

Table 4.1 *Evolution of gross product value*

Year	Value
1959	400,000
1970	825,000
1980	1,400,000
1986	1,900,000

Source: Institut Economique Agricole.

sufficiency exceeds 100 per cent, but this level is not reached for fruit (this includes a lot of mediterranean and exotic fruit). There is surplus production of meat (120 per cent), dairy products (122 per cent) and eggs (130 per cent).

This increase in productivity is partly a result of the intense mechanization of agriculture. For example, the number of combine harvesters increased from 611 in 1950 to 6,869 in 1989, i.e. one combine harvester for every 51 ha. of cereals. The average cultivated surface per labour unit in agriculture increased from 10.3 ha. in 1967–72 to 14.7 ha. in 1980–3.

After the introduction of the milk quota, more milk was produced on fewer farms with fewer cows. The number of dairy farms decreased from 44,809 in 1985 to 33,864 in 1989 (-26 per cent). The number of dairy cows decreased by 10 per cent, but deliveries to the dairy industry remained at the level of approximately 3.1 million tons per year. Similar increases affected other products.

Table 4.2 gives an overview of yield increases for some products.

Table 4.2 *Evolution of productivity in some selected products*

	Unity	1970	1985
Winter wheat	100 kg./ha	44.5	63.2
Sugar beet	100 kg./ha	474.5	489.0
Milk	1./cow/year	3,425	3,873

Source: Institut Economique Agricole

Industrialisation also increased. In 1955, only 34 per cent of the milk was sold to dairy plants, whereas the proportion had risen to 86 per cent by 1989: dairying on one's own farm has become the exception and the success of the 'farm butter' label and of 'farmers' markets' does not reverse this trend. It should also be noted that the agro-industry has undergone concentration: in 1950 there were 256 dairies, in 1986 only 58, forming five conglomerates (increasingly foreign-owned).

Increase in regional differences

There are noteworthy regional differences in Belgian agriculture: in 1970, the area of an average farm in Flanders was 5.81 ha. but in Wallonia it was 13.38 ha. In 1989, the figures were 10 and 25 ha. respectively. Flemish farms tend to be smaller: two-thirds of Belgian farms are situated in Flanders, which represents 44 per cent of the national agricultural territory.

There are also differences in the product field. 'Traditional' crops such as grassland, cereals and sugar beet remain proportionally more prevalent in Wallonia. 'Modern' crops such as horticulture and greenhouse crops, but especially crops that are not linked to the soil, e.g. intensive pig breeding have increasingly become a Flemish affair. These regional differences should not be confused with those related to the special support allocated to specific regions such as mountainous areas within the common agricultural policy. In Belgium, the regional differences resulting from the European policy were of a different nature.

The evolution is partly to be set against its historical background. The loamy soil of a part of Wallonia was especially appropriate for crops such as sugar beet and wheat, while cattle farming thrived in the region south of the Sambre and the Meuse. Flanders, more densely populated, had a tradition of market gardening for the nearby towns.

These existing differences were strengthened by divergent responses to the common agricultural policy. The Walloon farms increasingly concentrated their activities on those products for which intervention (price support) was strongest: cereals and milk. Flemish farms tended to privilege crops that, thanks to the opening of the markets, offered new possibilities: pig breeding, horticulture, even ornamental plant culture. In Flanders, with its tradition of small-scale production, the common agricultural policy did not offer prospects of large-scale farming of the crops in which Wallonia specializes. The alternative to disappearance was reconversion towards efficient production of crops with a growing market, notably thanks to the increased standard of living, but not subject to the same protective measures as milk and cereals. Small, even marginal farms could survive by reconverting to efficient production of high-added-value crops. This explains the development of horticulture and floriculture as a Flemish activity: 50 per cent of azaleas and 60 per cent of begonias produced in Europe come from Belgium.

Table 4.3 presents an overview of the regional distribution of some crops.

Greenhouse farming, an high-added-value activity, is almost exclusively situated in Flanders: the total area of greenhouses (including crops under plastic) increased from 1758 ha. in 1970 (Flanders/Wallonia: 97.8/2.2) to 1821 ha. in 1985 (Flanders/Wallonia: 97.7/2.3) (Van Haeperen 1987b).

Although farms tend to be smaller in Flanders and more geared

Table 4.3 *Evolution of regional distribution of selected crops (in per cent)*

		Flanders	Wallonia
'Traditional crops'			
Cereals	1970	45.1	54.9
	1985	35.9	64.1
Hay and meadows	1970	42.5	57.5
	1985	41.5	58.5
'Modern crops'			
Vegetables (open air)	1970	58.6	41.4
	1985	70.7	29.3
Fruit	1970	77.0	23.0
	1985	91.3	8.7
Pigs	1970	81.2	18.8
	1985	93.8	6.2

Source: Van Haeperen 1987b.

towards 'modern' crops, the general tendency of concentration can also be noted in this region. In the pig-breeding sector, the number of farms decreased by 28 per cent between 1985 and 1989. In 1987, the average number of pigs per farm was 221 (5,861,000 for the whole sector), but it had already reached 300 (a total of 6,654,000) by 1989. In 19 per cent of the farms there were more than 500 pigs: 68 per cent of the total. The average in the 500+ group was 1,093 pigs per farm.

We could also point to cultural differences between the regions to explain the differences: in Wallonia the role of public authorities (in this case the Belgian government as executor of the European policy) in modelling economic development is more generally accepted, whereas many Flemish farmers work within the efficient framework of an organization that has branches capable of supporting viable farms in developing their activities in modern crops by training, credit services and commercialization.

These regional differences partly explain why agricultural problems are perceived differently in the two regions, notably in relation to environmental issues: problems related to the insertion of agriculture into the local environment (e.g. the disposal of manure from non-soil-linked pig breeding) are different in the densely populated Flemish region (423 inhabitants per sq. km.) and the less densely populated Walloon region (192 inhabitants per sq. km.).

Internationalization

Before European integration, agriculture was developing within national borders. European integration meant that national borders were gradually replaced by international borders. One result is that Belgian farms have to be competitive in a much larger market. This offers possibilities but also challenges. Belgian pig-breeding farms have seized the opportunities of the European market and are exporting a considerable part of their produce. Belgian endive growers, on the other hand, have to face competition from their French colleagues, who are increasingly producing this traditional Belgian crop very efficiently.

Agriculture-related industry is becoming increasingly international. Concentration is taking place both with suppliers (e.g. of intermediate products or of equipment) and buyers of agricultural products. Farmers are facing international conglomerates, which seriously affects their bargaining position. Because of internationalization, international agreements have their repercussions for Belgian agriculture. First and foremost, there are the GATT negotiations. An agreement on decreases in agricultural support would surely be felt by many Belgian farmers. There are, however, other international agreements. Regulations on the imports of intermediate products such as cassava and sweet potatoes have an impact on the price structure of inputs for fattening plants. Agreements in the framework of the Lomé convention – for example on imports of beef – can have consequences for the competitiveness of some European products.

Belgian agriculture has become more vulnerable because of this internationalization: considerations of global policy have come to influence Belgian agriculture. At the same time, Belgium is sharing responsibility with other European countries for market distortions in Third World countries, for example by dumping practices, especially of cereals.

Environment

From all the problems related to agriculture, the environmental problem is the one which especially alarms public opinion. We mean here environmental problems in the broad sense: product quality (e.g. the use of hormones in meat production, pesticide residues in food), waste problems (e.g. the disposal of manure) and pollution (e.g. nitrate poisoning, the contribution to the creation of acid rain).

Production pressure – the need to survive in unprotected and consequently highly competitive surroundings – has undeniably contributed to the development of certain practices which are harmful to the environment. Specialization and increases in scale are some of the elements responsible for the erosion occurring in some regions of Belgium. In the loam region of central Belgium, ten tons per ha. of fertile top-soil are washed away every year. In some municipalities, measures have had to be taken to halt this development (Goeteyn 1989). The increased use of fertilizers also causes problems. In 1958, 341,000 tons of fertilizers (nitrogen, potash and phosphate) were applied on 1.66 million ha. By 1983, this volume had risen to 450,000 tons on 1.34 million ha. – an increase of 66 per cent per ha. The quality of the surface water and of the underground water has been negatively affected by the increased use of fertilizers.

European integration has indirectly contributed to an intensification of the environmental problems. On the other hand, however, the European Community has stimulated public discussion on the role of agriculture in environmental problems. It is expected that European anti-pollution measures will have beneficial effects in Belgium, too. Until recently, the big farmers' organizations were able to hush up or to deny the co-responsibility of agriculture in environmental problems such as acid rain.

Changes at farm level

Specialization

Farms have become increasingly specialized. The need for investments in any specific activity to yield the highest possible return leads to specialization in that activity. In 1988, according to EC criteria, 74.4 per cent of Belgian farms were specialized: the proportion of pig-raising farms decreased from 56 per cent of all Belgian farms in 1956 to 24 per cent in 1989, for example, while the total number of pigs quadrupled over the same period. Even within this sector, specialization is increasing: the breeding of piglets and the fattening of pigs became increasingly separate activities, located on different farms. After the severe outbreak of porcine fever of early 1990, the so-called 'closed farm', combining the different stages of pig raising and fattening, is again being propagated. The transport of pigs, often over large distances, from breeding farm to fattening plant, leads to a greater exposure to contamination. In this case, technical arguments (i.e. hygienic requirements) advocate against specialization, pursued for reasons of profitability.

New investments are increasingly directed towards equipments or buildings for one specific crop or activity such as flax-harvesting machines, installations for endive hydroculture, stables for dairy cows. This unavoidably leads to a certain rigidity in production: it becomes practically impossible to switch to other crops before the investment is paid off, even though the market might require so.

The most developed form of specialization is production on a contract basis: farmers contract with one specific agro-industrial firm to produce a certain crop or product. Examples are vegetable-growing for the canning industry and the fattening of pigs for the fodder industry. The pig-fattening sector is for 70 per cent 'integrated', the calves and spring chicken sectors for 90 per cent. Flax-growing in central Belgium is in most cases practised under contract with traders or industrialists from the Courtrai region.

Agricultural policy of the last decades has gradually transformed the farmer into a manager of a specialized small-scale enterprise. The management of this enterprise requires a high degree of specialization and technical training in order to perform efficiently and to survive in a difficult market.

Loan burden

In 1988, an average capital (soil, building and equipment) per farm of 9.7 million francs yielded a product value of 2.4 million francs. This ratio of 4:4 between capital and product value is reached in no other branch of the economy. In 1968, the figures were 2.4 million francs and 0.4 million francs respectively. In 1968, 37 per cent of the capital was property of the farmers. By 1988, this proportion had risen to 40 per cent. This makes agriculture not only the most capitalized but also the most autofinanced sector. The other side of the coin is the increasing loan burden. In 1968, 8 per cent of capital was loaned; by 1988, this rate had doubled to 16 per cent.

This loan burden creates problems in the short term: maintaining the viability of the farm can lead to a decreased living standard for the farmer's family. The farmer can be obliged to accept a certain decrease in living standard if this is the alternative to bankruptcy. But, also in the long term, this load burden causes problems: it becomes increasingly difficult for young farmers to buy a farm. At the same time, it becomes less interesting for older farmers to sell a fully equipped, modern farm, as the buyers cannot afford to pay the price. Towards the end of the farming career, the tendency is to decrease investments and even to start eating into capital. In any case, young farmers are faced with a heavy load burden, either for taking over a well-equipped — and thus expensive — farm or for modernizing an outdated one — even though the initial price might have been lower.

This problem is linked to the need for efficient production in a difficult market as well as to the family character of Belgian agriculture: the farmer is at the same time the main (or only) shareholder and manager of his company.

On a yearly basis, one to two per cent of the loans cannot be repaid, which leads to the forced sale of the farm. For a larger proportion, repayment causes heavy sacrifices, often in the living standard of the family. Some of the problems are personal — overestimation of capacity, wrong calculation of the value of the farm that is sold to a young farmer — but some stem from the conventional way of calculating the risk.

When studying the feasibility of a loan, the market is supposed to remain stable or to develop in the same way it has in the past. The common agricultural policy, however, can cause important changes in the objective conditions, for example by imposing quotas: failure to obtain a milk quota can cause heavy problems to farmers who are already deeply in debt.

Family income

The Belgian farm is a family farm, and, to a growing extent, a one-man farm. After the agricultural crisis of the last century, public authorities chose to stimulate Belgian agriculture, based on the flexible family farm. Almost all farm labour is supplied by the family: in 1983, out of 102,024 labour units on the professional farms, 74,293 were managers, 21,609 were members of the family and only 6,122 labour units came from outside the family. The last figure might be slightly higher because of the existence of 'black' seasonal labour, but the overall picture remains the same.

The common agricultural policy has an impact on the farmers' incomes: directly through interventions on prices and quota for certain crops and products, indirectly through the intensification of competition, the growing need to invest and, consequently, the increased loan burden. Government or European intervention in agriculture has become the rule rather than the exception.

The income of the farming population is a social problem, not so much because of the number of people affected (farmers represent only 2.4 per cent of the population) but because of its seriousness for individual families. From 1972/3—83 labour income in agriculture increased from 100 per cent to 195.9 per cent but comparable labour income in other sectors of economy increased from 100 per cent to 269.6 per cent. This means a relative decrease of income in agriculture of 27 per cent. Alternative employment in other sectors, envisaged when the common agricultural policy was initially worked out, has become increasingly hard to find because of persisting high unemployment or because of the lack of required skills in farmers. People are forced to remain in agriculture and to accept the unfavourable evolution of incomes.

The evolution of incomes in agriculture is more favourable in Flanders than in Wallonia. This difference has political consequences: in federal Belgium, agriculture is still a national responsibility. The divergent evolution gives way to demands in Wallonia to transfer responsibility for agriculture to the regional authorities. Some of the Walloon farmers feel that the national agricultural policy is more favourable for Flanders. This feeling is strengthened by the fact that for many years the minister of agriculture was (and still is) Flemish and that the companies belonging to the Flemish farmers' organization are particularly successful (in fact, part of their profit is made by trade with Walloon farmers).

Conclusion

Belgian agriculture has been fundamentally transformed, both qualitatively and quantitatively, in order to find its place in a competitive environment. However, the sector is still not 'stabilized': compared to agriculture in other north-west European countries, Belgian agriculture remains very vulnerable. Holland and the UK have maintained or even expanded their share of Europe's agricultural production, whereas Belgium's share is still slowly declining. The removal of agricultural surpluses, the product quality and the care of the environment, the repercussions of the integration of European agriculture into the world economy (the GATT negotiations) and the creation of direct income support could cause new shocks in agriculture.

European unification, however, should not be blamed for all the problems currently affecting Belgian agriculture. In the absence of European integration, opening up Belgian agriculture to international competition and adapting it to the desiderata of the agro-industry would probably have caused similar problems. The integration of farmers into the community, that used to be automatic, is increasingly being questioned, because of problems in agriculture: environmental problems, the price of agricultural surpluses, the consequences of agriculture for the European position towards GATT, the European position on agricultural imports from Third world countries, etc. Agriculture is becoming a topic for public debate. New orientations in agricultural policy will probably not be the result of mere consultation between authorities and farmers' leaders. The repercussions of agricultural problems on everyday life has awakened some of the population. Future integration of agriculture into society will probably have to be based not only on economic but also on social and environmental considerations.

Before European integration, agriculture was an economic activity as well as a rural lifestyle. After European integration, agriculture came to be seen as one branch of the economy, with the same needs of efficient production and expansion. The crisis agriculture is now going through, however, indicates that the mere criteria of productivity and profitability will not be enough to raise support for new policies. Social elements (the living standard of farmers and their families, the stability of producer prices), economic elements (the prices to be paid by consumers, but also the prices of capital and intermediate goods), elements of industrial policy (the development of agro-industry) and environmental considerations (product quality, pollution problems) all have to be taken into consideration when drafting an agricultural policy for the future.

The way agriculture becomes integrated into Belgian society will to a large extent be decided at European level. The involvement of Belgian farmers and consumers in this decision-making will give an indication of Europe's capability to realize a democratic policy elaboration.

References

Brown, G. C. (1990) 'Distributional aspects of CAP price support', *European Review of Agricultural Economics*, vol. 17-3, 289–301.

Demblon, D., J. Aertsen et al. (1990), *100 Jaar Boeren*, EPO, Berchem.

Goeteyn, L. (1989) 'Bodemerosie, een sluipend milieuprobleem', *Milieurama*, no. 7/8.

Mormont, M. and B. Van doninck (1992) 'La représentation des agriculteurs en Belgique', in B. Hervieu (ed.) *Les organisations professionnelles agricoles en Europe*, L'Harmattan, Paris.

Van Haeperen, J.-M. (1987a) 'Studie van de interne wijzigingen in de landbouw', *L.E.I. Publikaties*, no. 477, Studies no. 9.

Van Haeperen, J.-M. (1987b) 'Evolution comparée des structures de l'agriculture wallonne et flamande au cours de la période 1970–1985', *Publications de l'I.E.A. no. 481*, Etudes no. 13.

Chapter 5

Environmental policy

Luc Hens

European legislation

European environmental policy is essentially directed towards the establishment of directives which need to be implemented in the national legislations of the Member-State governments. For the environmental policy as a whole, only five directives exist: the import of whale products, the application of the convention on international trade in endangered species of wild fauna and flora, the Communities actions for the environment and the protection of woods against air pollution and on CFCs (chlorofluorohydro-carbons) damaging the ozone layer.

Until 1986 we faced the situation that *sensu stricto* the Communities were not supposed to establish an environmental policy. The original aim of the EC was the organization of the free-market system within the European 'Economic' Community. The 1957 Treaty of Rome, which sets out the powers and duties of the various institutions of the Community, does not mention environment. Because of the concern for the free market, the needs for a common environmental policy became clear from the early 1970s. Coordination of the national environmental legislations should avoid distortions of the free movements of products induced by different national standards (De Gucht and Nys 1987).

So Article 100 was used to accept the so-called 'harmonization directives. The most well-known of these are about what are considered to be dangerous products: pollution by gases from motor vehicles and noise pollution. Article 100 states that the Council of Ministers can approve directives which aim to unify these legislations of the Member States which have a direct influence on the EC or on the functioning of the common market. So the Council could only intervene when national rules which had or were presumed to have effect on the free market already existed.

As for the subjects which were not covered by Article 100, Article 235 of the EC treaty was brought into action. This Article makes it possible for the Council to accept directives on new powers to achieve

Community objectives. This can be done even though these powers were not included in the Treaty of Rome.

Gradually the Communities felt it necessary to implement an environmental policy. Since 1973 the Commission has submitted environmental action programmes. These only have organizational capacity and no real legal power. Specific environmental directives have also been decreed within the framework of the interpretation of Article 235.

So the legal basis of a justification for an EC environmental policy has never been properly established. As far as the procedure for the creation of environmental directives is concerned, there are even more difficulties. Directives were only put forward after a proposal from the independent and non-elected European Commission, while the Parliament only had an advising role. Directives also need to be decided unanimously by the Council of Ministers. As a consequence directives were developed only very slowly and were often characterized by many compromises (Reynders 1988).

The Single European Act (see Chapter 1) of 17 February 1986 effected many changes although not all problems were solved. This Act reviews the powers and the duties of the EC. It regulates not only the 1992 free market, but also deals explicitly with European duties on environmental matters. Moreover, the procedure for submitting European directives has changed.

In this new EC treaty there is an Article on the 'Environment'. The new Article 130R lists the main themes of European environmental policy: environmental quality, public health and the use of resources. The intention is to work on these themes based on the principles of preventive action, treatment at source and the polluter pays. It is also important to notice the intention that environmental protection should form an integrated part of all aspects of European policy.

Article 130R also contains elements which were necessary in order to find a political compromise between the individual Member States. A number of countries wanted particular points of special relevance for them to be explicitly mentioned. Great Britain, for instance, asked for attention to be given to the availability of scientific and technical data, the possible differences in environmental conditions in different regions and the costs of environmental policy. Poorer member states such as Greece and Ireland asked for attention to be paid to differences in economic and social developments in the different regions.

Article 130T, on the other hand, reflects the German and Danish wishes to open possibilities for more rigorous environmental standards, in spite of the European norm settings. These stricter standards are only tolerated when they do not interfere with the free-market principle.

The national states are still the ultimate decision-makers. According to Article 130S, the Council of Ministers can only accept an environmental directive by unanimous voting. The Council, however, can decide beforehand which decisions will be accepted by a qualified majority.

The European Parliament must be consulted on all environmental policy decisions. The Parliament as yet has no real decision-making powers. However, it plays an increasing role within the framework of Article 100A which deals with the harmonization of national environmental laws. Basically the Article aims to realize the internal free market. According to this Article, Parliament can also submit amendments directly. Another interesting new feature is that the final decision on a harmonization directive in the Council can be taken by a qualified majority. The Council, however, must always implement a high level of environmental protection. Nevertheless, it is possible that in the future individual member states will have more rigorous environmental standards, provided they do not coincide with a hidden protection of the national market.

Now the competence of the EC to adopt legislative measures for the protection of the environment and how is will proceed to do so are clear. This chapter evaluates how this competence is used. It is a fact that most environmental directives reflect the different national interests on any given subject. Too often most of the attention of the Council ministers is devoted to the economic implications of new environmental regulations. The interests of national industries and the free market aspects of competition are in general also matters of primary concern (De Pue 1983).

Environmental regulations are often part of 'package deals'. This means essentially that one member country is willing to accept a particular point, another country is willing to accept another element of the package. These factors to a large degree explain the inertia in environmental regulation at Community level and the fact that most standards are not sufficiently well-defined. Indeed, they reflect the compromise deals of 12 different countries. Moreover the Commission only pays small attention to themes with less of an economic implication such as nature conservation and the management of (semi)natural systems.

Belgian policy

It can be demonstrated that to a large extent Belgian environmental policy was inefficient and did not deal with the final aim of environmental policy: the quality of the environment. As to the management of the problems in most environmental fields (water, dangerous waste, soil, noise) only very little or no progress has been made. Relative success has been achieved in the field of air pollution where mainly industrial emissions have been reduced. The actual reduction of SO_2 emission values during the 1970s was 50 per cent due to the reduction of these emissions in neighbouring countries, mainly in the German Federal Republic.

An efficient environmental policy in Belgium is still lacking in spite of a growing general environmental consciousness and growing pressure on politicians. This can be demonstrated not only by the extremely bad quality of the Belgian surface waters and the far-reaching pollution pressures on the soil and groundwater. The implementation of an environmental policy also functions poorly. A good example of this is the permit policy. Permits are either non-existent or they are delivered 'à la tête du client' (according to the wishes of the client and not as a function of general environmental quality). Control on the functioning of these permits and environmental legislation in general is very poor. From the judicial court point of view, up to 95 per cent of the environmental cases are dismissed. Non-governmental environmental associations have no rights to complain about environment-damaging situations.

It is extremely difficult to obtain reliable information on the quality and actual status of the Belgian environment. Civil servants and members of environmental research centres fight shy of telling the truth. The few public reports are often characterized by irrelevant and outdated information. The Belgian citizen had no right to look at the permits. In cases of clear-cut violations of the law and obvious environmental damage, there were many examples of local authorities protecting the polluters. But, from 1 September 1991 the European directive on public access to environmental information was implemented in Flanders, and minimal and passive access possibilities now exist.

A global approach to Belgian environmental policy reveals that its inefficiency is at least partially related to a unique sectorial approach to environmental problems. For each compartment Belgium has a separate legal approach with separate permit procedures, separate control authorities and a separate administrative structure. There is no 'source'-related policy; there are only uncoordinated 'end of the line' approaches. There is no product policy, no substances-related policy and no policy of interference with production systems. These elements, however, are essential for the fundamental, 'source'-related management of pollution. As long as such a policy is absent, Belgium continues to transpose its environmental problems both in time and in space (the so-called law of 'maintenance of misery').

There is, however, a gradual process in favour of the establishment of an integrated environmental policy. The former Flemish Minister for Environmental Affairs, T. Kelchtermans, presented two drafts of an environmental management plan in which, for example, a special policy for different groups of polluters has been developed. Within the same framework an inter-university commission developed a global, integrated framework for environmental legislation. The aim is the development of a global legal framework in which the laws related to the different environmental compartments are coordinated. This framework must also provide guarantees of an efficient delivery of permits, public control and judicial prosecution.

Implementation of European policy

The execution of European environmental directives is a time-consuming process, as is the implementation of a directive into Belgian legislation. Indeed, it is not sufficient to have European directives: they must be converted into national laws and the control on the implementation of the national rules must be effective (Glasbergen 1989).

As for the implementation of environmental European directives, Belgium has a bad reputation. The Belgian government has been condemned on several occasions by the European Court of Justice because the state did not implement the directives in time. The Belgian legal defence was always concerned with the process of restructuring the state according to a more federal model. With this process of restructuring the state, a number of problems of regional competence on environmental matters are apparent. These arguments, however, were not accepted by the European Court of Justice. As a result the Belgian state was condemned for the first time on 1 February 1982 for only partial implementation of six directives. On 14 January 1990 this condemnation was repeated for four of these six directives, although two of them dated from 1975! As a consequence of the systematic non-implementation of environmental directives, the Belgian state was openly criticized by the Commissioner for the environment, Ripa di Meana.

It is remarkable that the national Belgian government is condemned for the non-implementation of directives which actually must be implemented by the regional authorities (Flemish, Walloon and Brussels). As a result of separation in the fields of competence between the national and the regional authorities, the state government has no power to intervene at regional level and to impose the implementation of the directives. On the other hand the regional authorities are often unwilling to implement the directives. They argue that the national state was involved in the negotiations on the contents at EC level, but they were not (David 1989).

However, the law on the restructuring of the Belgian state explicitly says that regional authorities should participate in international negotiations on matters of regional competence. Moreover, since the restructuring of the state on 8 August 1988, the regional authorities are obliged to implement directly (without participation of the national government) all European environmental directives. The national authorities are only allowed to provide standards in areas where no European regulations exist. It is a fact that the Brussels government particularly and to a lesser extent the Walloon and Flemish governments failed to implement the European directives till 1989.

In conclusion, Belgium systematically violates the European Treaty with 'constructive negligence'. The restructuring of the state did not foresee a structure taking care of the timely and complete implementation of the directives. This situation does not coincide with the contents of

Article 5 of the EC Treaty which states that member states should facilitate (and not make more difficult) the adoption of legislative measures and other duties. So Belgium not only systematically violates the Treaty but the violation is to some extent inherent in the actual state structures (Bocken 1986)! Therefore condemnations by the European Court are no solution. They only make clear the symptoms of the Belgian disease. Indeed, the Court lacks the instruments to confront this member state with effective sanctions when this state does not respond in a way which would accord with the international condemnation.

Moreover, the EC lacks the instruments to control the application of environmental directives in the different member states. Indeed, it is not sufficient when the directives are converted into national laws. These laws must also be working elements of the local environmental policy and efficiency in this area must be guaranteed by a suitable control system.

Most directives also include duty of information. On a regular basis, the national authorities must inform the Commission on the national application of the directive. As a rule Belgium does not fulfill these duties of information. This information, however, is of outstanding importance as it provides the Commission with a factual basis for the evaluation of the directives and the review of its environmental policy. This information is also of interest for the national non-governmental environmental associations. One reason for this is that they get access to information which as a rule is not normally accessible for them.

In 1990 the EC environmental service was enforced by new inspectors. The commission has also created an environmental bureau to manage a data bank with environmental quality data provided by the Member States. The European Parliament has insisted that this bureau should also control the quality of these data and should manage the on-site control of the implementation of the directives. Some Member States felt this as a negation of their sovereignty. So we can only wonder about the possibilities of the European civil servant overcoming the barriers he will be confronted with at the national/regional level.

It is, however, quite clear that the effective control of the local efficiency of the environmental directives will provide a lot of work. This point can be illustrated by the results of a survey by the 'Bond Beter Leefmilieu' (Vrijdaghs 1988). Within a period of six months, the 66 member associations of this organization reported 350 situations of non-compliance with the existing European environmental directives. It must be remarked, however, that probably due to its closed, somehow bureaucratic character, the European environmental policy is not very well known by large numbers of the population.

It is, however, useful to know that every attentive citizen can help the European environmental inspection in a simple way. The EC information paper published a standard sheet which can be used in situations of non-compliance with European regulations. Everyone can complain. Active participation in such a process can force the country to manage environmental regulations actively and positively (David 1989).

The need for a high quality, well-controlled EC environmental policy is now more important than ever before. This statement gets support from the situation we shall face with the open market at the end of 1992 and the threatening consequences of this situation for the quality of the environment. (Glasbergen 1989).

Conclusions

The implementation of environmental policy in Belgium is characterized by these main elements:

- Most of the currently existing aspects of environmental policy are the result of an extremely slow implementation of European directives.
- Some elements are the direct result of political pressure by the environmental movement: reduction of CFC emissions, titandioxide policy and burning of industrial waste in open seas are some examples.
- Environmental policy in essential fields such as water treatment, product policy and nature conservation is much less developed in Belgium as compared to neighbouring countries.
- The implementation of a globally planned environmental policy to replace the long-standing *ad hoc* approach has now been initiated in Flanders. The slow, hesitant management of this policy indicates that results might only be expected in the long term.
- In Wallonia and Brussels implementation of European directives was slower as compared to Flanders. Since 1989 the formal implementation of EC directives was improved.

Environmental policy by the Communities is a major stimulus for Belgian environmental policy. In view of the specific characteristics of the Belgian ecosystem (high population density, intensive bioindustry and agriculture, a high degree of industrialization) it is however very uncertain whether the implementation of European environmental directives alone will be able to keep the environment in a sustainable condition.

References

Bocken, H. (1986) *De grondwettelijke bevoegdheidsverdeling inzake leefmilieu*, Brussels, Story.

David, H. (1989) '1992 en het milieu', *Info-leefmilieu*, 4, 115.

David, H. (1989) 'Belgie miskent Europese spelregls', *Milieurama*, 6, 3.

De Gucht, K. and Nys, J. V. R. (1987) *Bescherming van de leefomgeving: een korte schets van de bevoegdheidsverdeling tussen Europa, Belgie en de regio's, en de stand van toepassing van het gemeenschapsrecht door Belgie*, Liberaal Studiecentrum.

De Pue, E. (1983) 'Het Europes milieurecht: een inleidende schets', *Info-Leefmilieu*, 4, 117–28.

Glasbergen, P. (1989) (ed.) *Milieubeleid, theorie en praktijk*, VUGA, 317.

Reynders, L. (1988) '1992 Milieuramp', *Milieurama*, 12, 11.

Vrijdaghs, L. (1988) *Naleving van de Europese milieurichtlijnen in Vlaanderen*, Bond Beter Leefmilieu vzw.

Chapter 6

Budgetary policy

Servaas Deroose and Jef Vuchelen

European economic integration has persistently paid more attention to monetary policy than to budgetary policy. To some extent, this derives from the primary and long-standing aim of stabilizing exchange rates among member countries, on which monetary policy has a large, direct and predictable impact. Budgetary policy does not have such a decisive and instantaneous effect on a variable that is crucial to the integration process. Therefore, we can expect that budgetary policy will always be less harmonized and unified than monetary policy. At least this is suggested by the institutional setting of monetary and budgetary policy within existing federal countries and is reflected in the discussion on economic and political integration (CEC 1989a and b; Eichengreen 1990; Robson 1987). This situation also yields a pure political advantage since it leaves the more technical monetary policy to 'technicians' whereas the elected policy-makers can handle fiscal policy to which the public is more sensitive.

This brings us to probably the most important reason for the hitherto quasi non-existence of budgetary integration in the European Community – national economic sovereignty. The major obstacle to budgetary integration is the political unacceptability for national governments to give up (even partly) the right to set taxes and to spend the revenue raised. These activities are seen as being close to the essence of sovereignty. However, this does not inhibit a certain degree of integration in the budgetary sphere, provided that a strong case is made on economic and/or political grounds for ceding some budgetary powers to a supra-national level and that a sufficient degree of political accountability is ensured. This is why budgetary integration has become such a relevant issue since the publication in early 1989 of the Report on Economic and Monetary Union in the European Community (the so-called Delors Committee report). The report discusses the necessary parallelism between monetary and budgetary integration and provides an instrument for budgetary power-sharing between the Community and the member countries: namely the principle of subsidiarity.

It is thus not surprising to find that in Belgium as in the other member countries, the Community as policy-maker has interfered much less in budgetary than in monetary policy. However, this does not imply a complete absence of any influence at all. The impact of the EC on macroeconomic policy in general and on budgetary policy in particular has been both direct and indirect. By the first channel we mean that fiscal policy instruments were directly affected by actions at the EC level, for instance through EC directives such as the conclusions of the ECO/FIN Council (June 1991) to abolish fiscal frontiers in the Community (i.e. the harmonization of VAT rates and excise duties). We use the word 'direct' to indicate that the influence is on the operation of budgetary policy. Indirect effects, on the other hand, operated mainly through the effects of the EC on the objectives of economic policy. Since the instruments are modified to attain objectives, there will be an effect on the instruments but it will be an indirect one. For instance, a decision to reduce the variability in the exchange rates will indirectly influence budgetary policy.

This chapter will provide a brief excursion into the impact of the EC on the conduct of budgetary policy in Belgium. In doing so, no quantitative assessment will be made. Not only do we not dispose of a benchmark against which to measure this impact, but, more fundamentally, the EC has influenced budgetary policy in the member countries, in many cases, so subtly that a quantitative assessment would hardly be feasible. Instead, the following sections will give some speculative feel for the budgetary impact of the EC in the past by surveying, inevitably selectively, the major policies and actions by which the Community since its inception has endeavoured to influence, directly or indirectly, budgetary policy in Belgium. In line with this book's historical approach, the analysis is primarily confined to the first three decades of European integration. Recent developments, whose impact is still very speculative, are thus not dealt with.

The objectives of budgetary policy

The traditional objectives of budgetary policy are related to its allocation, distribution and stabilization functions. Tax and expenditure instruments should theoretically be used in such a way as to close the gap between objectives and the present situation. Effects from the EC could then proceed through changes in the objectives of budgetary policy.

The process of economic integration in itself leads to a loss of freedom in the selection of objectives. This is quite obvious with respect to monetary policy and implies, for instance, giving up the inflation target. Indeed, when the goal is to keep the exchange rate fixed, the inflation rate can no longer differ significantly from the rate in the major trading partner(s). To the extent that inflation is also an objective of budgetary policy (for instance, inflation is a tax on financial assets so that it can be used in redistribution policies), the integration process affects budgetary policy targets. Another example derives from the knowledge that with more intense trade relations between member countries, the importance of the competitive position increases. Integration therefore affects objectives whose achievement might jeopardize a country's competitiveness. Clearly, the objective of a more equal income distribution, a goal traditionally pursued in Belgium, implies progressive income-tax rates. The costs of these policies, as measured by the decline in international competitiveness, are likely to increase along with stronger trade integration. We can thus expect that redistribution objectives will be less actively pursued or even abandoned. The recent decline in marginal income-tax rates in Belgium, pursuant to similar moves in the major industrialized countries, illustrates this quite well.

As a result of the intensification of economic relations between the EC members, objectives therefore will tend to converge within the Community even in the absence of any specific action taken at the Community level (this will similarly influence policy instruments). However, the economic weight of the countries is not identical in the Community, inevitably causing convergence efforts in some countries to be larger than in others. Smaller countries normally have to adjust their targets more to those of the larger countries. For Belgium, a small open economy, this essentially means that the objectives pursued ought to be made consistent with those of the main trading partner, i.e. Germany. The lower degree of freedom for setting objectives experienced by smaller member countries might be compensated by two elements. First, in many cases they can benefit from a free-rider behaviour in pursuing objectives at the Community level. Second, being of minor importance for the overall situation in the Community, other member countries of Community institutions might adopt a less-demanding attitude when assessing the economic performance of smaller member countries.

Note, however, that we talk about convergence, not equalization or harmonization. The requirements for monetary policy are more stringent. The explanation is that fiscal policy, most of the time, only has an indirect effect on variables which are important for the relationships between the member countries. Furthermore, some asymmetries exist. A restrictive as well as an expansionary monetary policy will rapidly result in foreign exchange market problems because pressures for a devaluation or revaluation will develop. However, an expansionary fiscal policy will not lead to exchange market pressures when the budget and the balance of payments show a surplus.

The previous analysis illustrates the difficulty of evaluating the effect of the EC on national objectives of budgetary policy. Furthermore, objectives of economic policy are almost never made explicit and do not quantify in a unique way (for instance, how do we measure income inequality?). We must also take into account that objectives change over time. As mentioned above, the objective of more equality in the distribution of income had much more weight in the 1970s than in the 1980s. A similar argument concerns the full-employment target. Note, however, that, in principle, shifts in objectives are reflected in changes in instruments. We now turn to that analysis.

Instruments of budgetary policy

Direct influence

It would be surprising if the process of integration had not affected the use of economic policy instruments at the national level. This occurred through the *abolition* of certain tools (such as some types of subsidies) and the change in the reaction of economic agents and markets to policy measures (constraints are modified). An example of this last channel is the increased international mobility of labour and capital which might increase the cost of a non-alignment of instruments relative to partner countries.

The burgeoning literature on international tax coordination clearly demonstrates that economic integration considerably reduces the domestic playing-field of national tax authorities. In view of the creation of an internal European market in 1993, the abolition of fiscal frontiers will have significant repercussions on the level and structure of tax revenues in several member countries. In anticipation of '1992', some of them (Belgium among them) have already started to adjust their tax systems. The budgetary impact of the latest agreement of 'indirect tax harmonization in the Community' (June 1991) is generally estimated to be weak in Belgium's case. It would imply a certain reduction in VAT receipts largely compensated by an increase in revenues from higher excise duties. On the other hand, given increasingly integrated and liberalized capital markets worldwide, a policy of high taxation of capital income appears to be potentially very costly.

However, *new* instruments have also been created and we can expect that, as a result of coordination, some instruments will show a higher efficiency. By new instruments we do not mean the switch of, for example, turnover-taxes to VAT, but new taxes and expenditures. One important example for Belgium is the withholding of tax on capital income for residents which was introduced in 1962 with the argument that it would be required for the European integration process. However, it took more than 25 years to start the discussion on this problem at the EC level. The 1985 White Paper recognized the need for a certain harmonization of taxation of income from capital. For several reasons, the Commission's proposal (1989a) for introducing a Community-wide 15 per cent withholding of tax was disapproved. The alternative to tax harmonization, a strengthened assistance among tax authorities in order to fight tax evasion, gained growing support. This incited the Belgian authorities to reduce the withholding tax to 10 per cent (from 25 per cent) in March 1990. In the meantime, the Belgian economy suffered as a result of the premature introduction of the withholding tax. We can indeed argue that this withholding tax was partly responsible for the existence of a two-tier exchange market (the latter was abolished in May 1990 in accordance with the deadline set by the third Community directive on capital movements (1 July 1990, i.e. the start of Stage One of Economic and Monetary Union)). Experience suggests that these controls have not been successful in isolating domestic financial markets in the long run, nor in preventing the export of financial capital, resulting in economic welfare losses. This example illustrates that there might also be costs involved when a country 'anticipates' too rapidly the possible introduction of an EC instrument.

The main example of the EC having had a clear effect on the instruments related to budgetary policy concerns the switch to the VAT-system, operational in Belgium since 1971. As such, this was clearly very helpful in the realization of the European integration process. However, no other fiscal instrument became as harmonized as the VAT-system, illustrating that in the taxation field no global approach has been pursued. This follows clearly from the provisions on taxation in the amended Treaty: only the various forms of indirect taxation are considered (Article 99) since these policy instruments are more likely to affect intra-Community trade. This seems to imply that national power to set rates for direct taxation and social security contributions are considered less harmful for the integration process. While to a certain extent this is related to the priority given to trade integration, it is not clear to what extent this also reflects a demand-side view of the economic system (policies are directed towards international trade flows, not to the production of goods and services) or a belief that direct taxation can easily be harmonized through the market, assuming that politicians react when differences in tax rates or tax bases affect the behaviour of economic agents.

Concerning government expenditure, no specific influence from the EC can be detected. There were directives concerning such matters as public procurements and state aids, but these relate more to the field of competition and industrial policy than to budgetary policy, even in a broad sense.

Indirect influence

Thus far, we have to admit that the costs and benefits that are directly linked to the effect of the EC on budgetary policy have been rather flimsy. This derives from the fact that until very recently no clear integration objective was directly related to budgetary policy.

Notwithstanding the integration and harmonization process, countries still have the opportunity, within the constraints imposed by the markets, to pursue their 'own' goals with budgetary policy, such as, for example, a more equal income distribution. This 'freedom' of the budgetary authorities, however, is not absolute. Despite a *de jure* sovereignty of national budgetary policies, implying the formal command over policy instruments, smaller member countries in particular do not have a *de facto* complete control over budgetary developments. The ability to achieve specified objectives by the skilful manipulation of instruments is, for instance, limited by the external constraint. The macroeconomic aspects of the EC dimension of budgetary policy were therefore not at all irrelevant. We must take into account that budgetary policy can have an effect on the exchange-rate target through, *inter alia*, the financing of the budget deficit. More specifically, an excessive monetary financing of the budget deficit will result in foreign exchange market problems and put pressure on monetary policy. In addition, excessive budget deficits, even when not financed by money creation, are likely to interfere with the proper conduct of a stability-oriented monetary policy. For these reasons, an eye has to be kept on the magnitude as well as on the method of financing the budget deficit. Since Belgium had and has a problem with these two indicators, the additional international pressure to consolidate its public finances was most welcome. It is here, we believe, that the most significant impact of the EC on budgetary policy must be found. *Two channels* can be distinguished: on the one hand, what can be called the demonstration-effect of integration and, on the other, the EC machinery for coordinating budgetary policies in the Community.

As regards the first channel, the *demonstration-effect of integration*, it is a widely perceived phenomenon that a country participating in an integration process often takes the performance or policy actions of the other members as a reference for guiding its own policies. In the Belgian context, this demonstration-effect is clearly exemplified by the choice of the average of the Community as a presumptive reference for the Belgian budget deficit. In the first half of the 1980s when the budget deficit had increased to an unsustainable level (see table 6.1), arguments were needed to persuade the public to accept restrictive moves in budgetary policy. That the Belgian budget deficit was much larger than the Community average was a useful argument. Hence, between 1981 and 1985, the quantitative goal of budgetary policy was the average budget deficit of the EC member countries. The Belgian government never clearly explained the economic rationale behind this policy goal (the need for greater convergence as advocated by the EC was never alluded to) or what would happen if its divergent budgetary position continued or worsened. The implicit message of the policy-makers seemed to be that then even more painful measures would have to be taken. EC membership therefore played an important role in justifying the gradual shift in the budgetary stance since 1981.

Table 6.1 *Main public finance indicators in Belgium and the EC (as a percentage of GDP)**

		Level				Change		
		1973	1982	1985	1991	73–82	82–85	85–91
1. Gross public debt	B	64.2	97.4	119.8	129.4	33.2	22.4	9.6
	EC	37.4	50.3	59.1	62.0	12.9	8.8	2.9
	B-EC	26.8	47.1	60.7	67.4	20.3	13.6	6.7
2. Net lending (+) or net borrowing (−) of gen. government	B	−3.3	−11.0	−8.5	−6.4	−7.7	2.5	2.1
	EC	−1.1	−5.5	−5.2	−4.3	−4.4	0.3	0.9
	B-EC	−2.2	−5.5	−3.3	−2.1	−3.3	2.2	1.2
3. Direct taxes	B	13.5	19.8	19.5	16.5	6.3	−0.3	−3.0
	EC	9.8	11.8	12.3	12.8	2.0	0.5	0.5
	B-EC	3.7	8.0	7.2	3.7	4.3	−0.8	−3.5
4. Indirect taxes	B	12.3	12.3	11.8	11.8	0.0	−0.5	0.0
	EC	12.3	12.7	12.9	13.1	0.4	0.2	0.2
	B-EC	0.0	−0.4	−1.1	−1.3	−0.4	−0.7	−0.2
5. Social security contributions	B	11.5	13.0	14.7	14.8	1.5	1.7	0.1
	EC	11.3	14.4	14.6	14.6	3.1	0.2	0.0
	B-EC	0.2	−1.4	0.1	0.2	−1.6	1.5	0.1
6. Government transfers	B	19.1	25.2	24.3	22.2	6.1	−0.9	−2.1
	EC	15.9	21.2	21.4	21.3	5.3	0.2	−0.1
	B-EC	3.2	4.0	2.9	0.9	0.8	−1.1	−2.0
7. Interest payments	B	3.4	9.3	10.8	10.9	5.9	1.5	0.1
	EC	1.9	4.1	5.0	5.1	2.2	0.9	0.1
	B-EC	1.5	5.2	5.8	5.8	3.7	0.6	0.0

* 1973: EC without Greece and Portugal.

Source: Commission of the European Communities

The *EC machinery* regarding convergence of economic policy is stipulated in Title II or Part Three of the Treaty of Rome (conjunctural policy: Article 103; short-term economic measures: Articles 104—109). Despite these Treaty provisions and the creation of five policy-making committees, until the mid-1970s, macroeconomic policy coordination in the Community mainly took the form of a reciprocal exchange of information about national developments and policy intentions (Mortensen 1989). In fact, the potential gains from tighter forms of policy coordination were largely disregarded. In addition, already in this period, EC policy actions were mainly directed towards the monetary and financial situation in order to ensure an equilibrium on the balance of payments and to maintain confidence in the currency. It was only in the wake of the first oil crisis and in the mood of international Keynesian demand-management that more serious endeavours were undertaken to coordinate macroeconomic policies in the Community. It led to the adoption of the 1974 Council Decision on Economic Convergence (74/120/EEC) and its associated directive on Stability, Growth and Full Employment (74/121/EEC). The major novelty in the budgetary field was the provision of a yearly Council examination (in the second quarter) devoted to the fixing of quantitative budgetary guidelines for the member countries. In the EC framework, coordination of economic policies meant joint and interdependent actions, but without real direct legislative powers. Since 1974, in the budgetary sphere, the EC has operated through guidelines, opinions and recommendations. In designing their policies, member countries could accept, amend or reject the 'advice' contained in these Community documents. However, through the monitoring of economic policies of the member countries in the Monetary Committee and the Economic Policy Committee, their objectives were to enhance the effectiveness of this advice.

The enhanced coordination of economic policies in the Community after the first oil crisis has undoubtedly exerted some constraint on the conduct of national budgetary policies. Nevertheless, many observers believe that this constraint was more often apparent than real. In this respect, they point to the disappointing record of the budgetary guidelines as compared to budgetary outcomes (see table 6.2) and to the discontinuation of the formulation of these guidelines in 1987. In addition, neither in Belgium nor in some other member countries did the instruments provided for in these texts guard against a derailment of public finances in the late 1970s and early 1980s. However, it would be an exaggeration to conclude that these legal dispositions have not worked at all. First, we should not overlook the indirect and invisible character of this form of coordination. Second, despite these provisions, the degree of freedom of national budgetary authorities has remained largely unchallenged. Third, and most importantly, there is ample ground to argue that without actions at the Community level, public finances in Belgium would have unmistakably worsened even more, as the following *two examples* suggest.

Table 6.2 *Comparison of guidelines and out-turns of central government budget balance for Belgium (as a percentage of GDP)*

	1974	1975	1976	1977	1978	1979	1980	1981	1982	1983	1984	1985	1986	1987
1 Guidelines	−4.2	−3.6	−4.6	−4.7	−6.4	−6.8	−7.0	−6.4	−9.4	−11.1	−11.5	−10.6	−9.6	−7.8
2 Out-turn	−3.5	−5.1	−5.8	−6.2	−6.6	−6.9	−8.6	−13.4	−12.8	−12.8	−11.9	−11.3	−10.8	−9.4
3 Difference (1–2)	−0.7	1.5	1.2	1.5	0.2	0.1	1.6	7.0	3.4	1.7	0.4	0.7	1.2	1.6

Source: Commission services.

First, Belgium had the doubtful honour of being the first and only member country to receive a Commission Recommendation pursuant to Article II of Council Decision (74/120/EEC). This occurred in June 1981: the main reason was developments in public finances and wages which were highly inconsistent with a proper functioning of the EMS. On the budgetary side, the Commission recommended that the Belgian authorities implement a rigorous policy and suggested a list of specific measures (CEC, *European Economy*, no. 10, 1981).

The Belgian Prime Minister, who had already been asked by his European colleagues in March 1981 to take the required measures, could not persuade his government to change the course of economic policy and resigned. It was only at the end of 1981 that a new government slowly started to reduce the budget deficit and to remedy the other imbalances in the Belgian economy which had developed since the mid-1970s. A devaluation of the Belgian franc by 8.5 per cent within the EMS in February 1982 was, however, inevitable.

This Belgian case is a convincing example of how peer EC pressures may ultimately be effective in forcing member countries to adjust their policies. It should be emphasized that it was primarily the discipline of the EMS which compelled Belgium to accept a drastic change in economic and budgetary policies. Preoccupation with budgetary developments appeared to be of only secondary importance. The same can be said of the spectacular U-turn in Mitterand's economic policy in 1983.

Second, since 1982 the Community has produced several reports on budget discipline, the restructuring of public expenditure and tax reform. The 'Cooperative Growth Strategy for More Employment', launched in 1985 by the Commission, fitted the re-orientation of budgetary policy into a coherent economic framework. The self-feeding process of excessive budget deficits, high interest payments and accumulating public debt (the so-called 'snowball effect') was also extensively studied. In many of these documents, the Belgian situation served as an example not to be followed. These documents and the confidential debates in the Monetary Committee and the Economic Policy Committee must surely have influenced budgetary policy thinking and actions in Belgium. On many occasions, they have contributed to preparing the ground for Belgian authorities to enact new policy measures (e.g. the Belgian response to the worldwide use of supply-side policies).

While EC budgetary policy advice with respect to Belgium was generally accurate and instrumental in speeding-up the desired shifts in economic policy, the EC, however, was not unerring in its policy prescriptions. An illustration of a less timely and less well-suited policy move was undoubtedly the 'concerted action' decision of July 1978, linked, it should be added, to the Bonn Summit of the G7 countries. It aimed at achieving a higher economic performance through concerted and differentiated fiscal stimuli by the member countries. While the

Council Decision recognized the build-up of budgetary imbalances in Belgium, it nevertheless unambiguously recommended a fiscal boost for Belgium. The macroeconomic benefits of this concerted action were nil. On the contrary, in retrospect its costs appeared high as it seemed to have functioned as the beginning of a five-year period of unbridled budgetary profligacy in Belgium.

Peer pressure exerted by the EC machinery has recently intensified and is expected to do so increasingly in the future. The overall unsatisfactory results of the 1974 Decision on Economic Convergence and the enhanced needs for greater economic convergence during stage one of Economic and Monetary Union called for a new institutional framework for the coordination of economic policies in the Community. Consequently, a new convergence decision was adopted by the ECO/FIN Council in March 1990. 'Multilateral surveillance' constitutes the core element of the new decision. It means a regular, at least twice a year, in-depth examination of economic conditions, prospects and policies in the member countries and is intended increasingly to result in agreed policy commitments by each Member State. Special emphasis is placed on the surveillance of budgetary policies, implying a periodic review of the budgetary situation in the member countries, especially the size and the financing of budget deficits, before the national authorities start with the fiscal policy planning procedure. At the July 1991 multilateral surveillance exercise, the ECO/FIN Council requested the Member States to develop and communicate their medium-term adjustment programmes by the end of October 1991. Member States should clearly commit themselves to these convergence programmes. At the Community level, the programmes will be appreciated, discussed and finally endorsed.

Conclusions

A small open economy like that of Belgium needs to adjust its policies to those of its main trading partners. Without such adjustments, economic performance will falter. When belonging to a group of countries striving for more economic and monetary integration among them, speedy adjustment to external circumstances is all the more necessary. The need to link policies with those of the dominant Member State(s) does not imply, however, that all tools should be attuned completely. Although it is generally accepted that monetary policy autonomy needs to be surrendered much more than budgetary policy, some convergence inevitably also needs to take place in the budgetary sphere. Even today, however, it is not clear what degree of national budgetary sovereignty is compatible with a move towards economic and monetary union. The discussion on the budgetary aspects of the Delors report illustrates this well. This indicates that there does not seem to be a universally accepted

Table 6.3 *Belgium: contribution to and payments received from EC budget (ECU million)*

	1981	1982	1983	1984	1985	1986	1987	1988	1989	1990
1. Contribution to EC own resources	990.5	1148.3	1215.9	1238.3	1292.6	1448.1	1702.6	1833.5	1807.2	1763.7
(% of total)	(5.5)	(5.4)	(5.3)	(5.0)	(5.0)	(4.4)	(4.8)	(4.5)	(4.1)	(4.3)
2. Annual payments received*	597.9	649.3	735.5	840.1	1070.0	1164.2	985.4	838.5	683.3	989.8
(% of total)	(3.9)	(3.6)	(3.4)	(3.5)	(4.3)	(3.8)	(3.2)	(2.3)	(1.9)	2.7)

* For the period under consideration, these amounts are based on a geographical distribution of about 88 percent of total budgetary payments.

Source: Court of Auditors, Annual report concerning the financial year 1985 (OJ C 321, 15.12.1986) and financial year 1990 (OJ C 324, 13.12.1991).

view on the relationship between economic integration on the one hand and taxes, government expenditure or even budget deficits and public debt on the other. This explains the difficulty in evaluating the impact of the EC on Belgian budgetary policy. In periods of high budget deficits, this impact will certainly be more substantial than otherwise. However, we have to admit that since the 1960s, Belgium has persistently experienced a high deficit compared to the other EC member countries and that EC pressure has only marginally helped to remedy this chronic disease. Nevertheless, we believe that without the EC, budgetary indiscipline would have been even larger in Belgium.

When during the first three decades of European integration the EC dimension did not constitute an emphatic constraint on the design and implementation of national budgetary policies, at least not in Belgium, prospects are that in the years ahead EC membership will fundamentally alter the nature and degree of budgetary autonomy enjoyed by member countries. Questions pertaining to whether, how, to what extent and at what stage national budgetary policies need to be constrained in the process leading towards EMU have been put into the forefront with the publication of the Delors Committee report in early 1989 and the subsequent decision to embark on stage one of EMU on 1 July 1990 and, in December 1990, to instigate two Intergovernmental Conferences (IGC) to frame EMU and political union within the EC Treaty. Without prejudging the decisions which will eventually be taken at the IGC, it is widely accepted that further progress towards EMU will influence national budgetary policies in at least three important ways: (see CEC 1990, particularly chapter 5). First, it will change the way public finance is used as an *instrument* of economic policy (e.g. enhanced stabilization role in case of country-specific disturbances, institutionalized constraint on the size of budget deficits and/or public debt). Second, it will *directly* influence the ability of national governments to levy taxes and to spend (e.g. the loss of seigniorage revenue, temporary or permanent decline in the cost of borrowing). Third, through increased competitive pressures on governments it will *indirectly* impact on national decisions about public spending and revenues.

This chapter would be incomplete if not even a passing reference was made to the costs and benefits of EC membership in financial terms. Table 6.3 shows, for some years, the contribution of Belgium to the resources of the Community as compared with the payments from the EC budget made to Belgium. According to this table, EC membership was not directly beneficial to the Belgian budget. In 1990, the Belgian contribution to the EC budget amounted to 1.764 m. ECU while it received only 990 m. ECU. This table also shows that the loss from the budget has been growing since 1987, because of shifts in EC policies and new budgetary provisions. However, based on only 88 per cent of total budget payments, this table presents a somewhat biased view on the net budget position for Belgium. Estimates based on total payments suggest that on average Belgium received about 6 per cent of budget payments over the period 1985–8, resulting in a 'net winners' position (CEC 1989b). Moreover, such financial calculi of EC membership have a limited significance. Gains or losses of membership need to be assessed on a broader basis than provided by the budget. Apart from the overall economic effects, the budget approach ignores the net benefits accruing to Belgium for hosting the major part of the European institutions.

References

CEC *Annual Economic Reports*, various.

CEC (1985) *Completing the Internal Market, the White Paper*, COM(85)310.

CEC (1989a) *Tax Measures to be Adopted by the Community in Connection with the Liberalization of Capital Movements*, COM(89)60 Final, Brussels.

CEC (1989b) *The Community Budget: The Facts in Figures*, 1989 edition, Brussels.

CEC (1990) 'One Market, One Money', *European Economy*, no. 44, Luxemburg.

Committee for the Study of Economic and Monetary Union (1989) *Report on Economic and Monetary Union in the European Community*, Delors Committee report, Commission of the European Communities, Luxemburg.

Eichengreen, B. (1990) 'One Money for Europe? Lessons from the US currency Union', *Economic Policy*, no. 10.

Mortensen, J. (1989) *Macroeconomic Policy in the Community: Federalism v. Coordination: Where do we stand?*, CEPS, Brussels.

Robson, P. (1987) *The Economics of International Integration*, Allen & Unwin, London.

Chapter 7

Monetary policy

Marc Quintyn and Jef Vuchelen

As a small open economy that heavily depends on international trade (see Chapter 8), Belgium has real advantages in stabilizing the price of the currencies of its main trading partners. These benefits not only derive from an increase in international trade, but are also related to economic and financial policy. We can indeed argue that policies will gain credibility when economic agents expect the fixed exchange rates to persist, since this puts constraints on the instruments. Belgium is one of the few industrialized countries that has never experimented with an independently floating currency since the breakdown of the Bretton Woods system.

There exist in practice many possibilities for implementing a fixed exchange-rate policy. EC membership and the neighbourhood of a country with a solid reputation on economic policy, has led to the situation that Belgium has, for almost two decades now, been pursuing a policy of stabilizing the DEM exchange rate. First, within the framework of the European 'snake' and, since 1979, within the EMS. We should, however, admit that the policy, for reasons explained below, has not been completely successful. For a small country such as Belgium, the stabilization of the price of the currency of a large country such as Germany, has drastic consequences for the conduct of monetary policy. For instance, Belgian monetary policy, to a large extent, has to mirror the monetary policy pursued by its large and financially powerful neighbour. This conclusion has been drawn and accepted by the Belgian authorities. However, fiscal and income policies will also have to be aligned, to a certain extent, to the German ones. This has not occured and it has led to too much strain on the monetary policy and to the partial failure of the 'hard currency' policy.

The loss of freedom in pursuing independent macroeconomic policies can be considered the price the Belgian monetary authorities had to pay for the 'purchase' of credibility. This demonstrates that the economic agents interpreted the European exchange-rate arrangements as a more convincing commitment than nationally stated goals. It illustrates that the

BEF did not (or does no longer?) belong to the fundamentally strong European countries.

We will not discuss whether the (historical) choice for a fixed exchange-rate regime has been the right one, since there is no realistic alternative. We must also consider that the exchange-rate mechanisms were part of the European integration process which also has a purely political dimension. This implies that a complete analysis of the gains and losses of EC membership for the conduct of monetary policy in Belgium is, partly, without practical relevance. We will therefore restrict ourselves to a discussion of the nature of and the extent to which constraints are imposed on monetary policy and then move on to an overview of the implications of the hard-currency option for other macroeconomic policies.

Monetary policy constraints in Belgium

Belgium has persistently been a member of the European exchange rate arrangements which have been organized over the past 20 years. These aimed for less volatility of the bilateral European exchange rates after the breakdown of the Bretton Woods system. The exchange-rate systems, essentially the 'snake' and the EMS, have evolved so as to be dominated by West Germany. As a result, the policy aim of the Belgian monetary policy has been to stabilize the DEM exchange rate. Since West Germany has shown a tendency for an appreciation of its currency, the Belgian exchange-rate policy has been labelled 'hard-currency policy'. The practical policy result is that the monetary policy of the Bundesbank needs, to a large extent, to be copied by the Belgian central bank. Furthermore, the exchange rate is an intermediary target of economic policy, so the final policy goals of West Germany, such as low inflation, low interest rates and low rates of increase in labour costs have also become the goals of the Belgian policy-makers.

This loss of freedom with respect to monetary policy actions should not be considered as a cost imposed on Belgium by the EC because it is very likely that, even without the EC, the country would have linked its currency to the DEM. So Belgium would in any case have lost its policy autonomy. We could even argue that there are some benefits associated with the fact that the link is made through European exchange-rate arrangements. Indeed, these systems imply some form of coordination that may allow Belgium (and other countries that are in a similar situation *vis-à-vis* the DEM) to exert some 'influence' on German policies. Without this coordination, no such possibility would exist.

The impact on monetary policy does not imply that the Belgian monetary authorities lost their policy autonomy entirely. In reality they still allow a limited degree of freedom, brought about by capital movements that are not perfectly interest-elastic, by the width of the intervention margin and by the existence of a dual-exchange market. Recently the limited autonomy has been further reduced by the abolition of the dual-exchange market (March 1990) and the stronger link (smaller intervention margin) to the Deutschmark (May 1990). However, whether the room for manoeuvre can usefully be exploited for policy purposes may be questioned. Anyway, it will not allow a different policy, as such a policy would result in currency speculation, interventions and, eventually, devaluations; this outcome would clearly be in contradiction with the goal of a fixed exchange rate.

With regard to the conclusion on the dependence of the Belgian on the German monetary policy, some additional observations have to be made. First, the dominance of German policy has increased over the years, mainly as a result of higher international capital mobility, the gradual abolition of exchange controls, increased integration in the EC and the decision by the Belgian authorities to strengthen the link with the DEM. Second, as a result of the Belgian withholding of tax, Belgian investors have become, over the years, more sensitive to international financial variables.

Third, as noted, some degree of freedom was gained through the existence of a dual exchange market without, however, allowing Belgium to deviate substantially from international interest-rate trends. Its benefits are rather to be found in the fact that it served as a cushion for speculative attacks. Thus, no real structural freedom for monetary policy has been obtained through this two-tier market, but the system has allowed monetary policy to be independent of short-term temporary exchange market events. The period 1979–82, a period of heavy speculative attacks, is in this respect very illustrative: without a dual exchange market, the central bank would have needed to raise the interest rate much more than it actually has.

This can be illustrated by the difference in the notation of the US dollar on both markets (see table 7.1). Note, however, that the data reported in table 7.1 conceal the short term since they are yearly averages: the maximum daily difference observed amounted to more than 16 per cent. The dual exchange rate did therefore offer the central bank a limited degree of freedom. Alternatively, however, we can argue that the existence of a dual exchange-rate system delayed the necessary devaluation. Thus a unified exchange market could have put more pressure on the authorities to prevent a devaluation by appropriate policy actions or to devaluate earlier than February 1982. A positive answer to this question would still have to be interpreted cautiously because the success of a devaluation requires appropriate income and budgetary policies and it is not clear whether a switch in these policies would have been possible before 1982. So, all in all, this system has never served as a substitute for monetary policy but merely as a complement to it. Finally, it should be emphasized that, useful though this system may have been as a complementary instrument, its role has become very residual

Table 7.1 *Percentage difference between the free and the official US dollar rate, annual average of daily data, 1974–1990 (2m)*

1974	2.11
1975	2.72
1976	2.28
1977	0.14
1978	1.49
1979	2.83
1980	1.44
1981	6.03
1982	7.34
1983	1.72
1984	1.49
1985	0.51
1986	0.87
1987	0.62
1988	0.68
1989	0.20
1990 (2m)	0.00

Source: National Bank of Belgium.

over the last few years. This is, among other things, mainly because of the growing integration of international financial markets and the EMU movements; the two exchange markets were unified on 5 March 1990.

In sum, Belgian monetary policy is heavily constrained by its choice to stabilize the DEM-exchange rate. Such a choice was, however, unavoidable, so the costs involved should not really be taken into account.

Implications for other macroeconomic policies

We have difficulty in assessing the consequences of the 'hard' currency option for the coordination between monetary and other macroeconomic policies, for instance fiscal, income policy, etc. Although monetary policy is primarily responsible for the maintenance of a fixed exchange rate, other policies may not thwart this aim, otherwise too much strain will be put on monetary policy. So, since the monetary authorities can only control the nominal exchange rates, monetary policy has to be supplemented by other policies to allow a stabilization of the real exchange rate. This rate is especially relevant for international trade. This is illustrated in the following paragraphs.

An expansionary fiscal policy, for instance, will, when the stabilization of the exchange rate imposes a restrictive monetary policy, not only fuel the current account deficit, and negatively affect expectations and policy credibility, but it will also lead to an increase in the deficit, public debt and probably taxes. All this will affect interest rates, unemployment and growth unfavourably. Exchange market participants will deduct from this course of events that the parity no longer reflects economic fundamentals. This illustrates that the traditional textbook mechanism whereby a higher budget deficit and the ensuing interest rate rise attracts foreign capital, is not functioning in the medium term. Indeed, the higher interest rate will have to be balanced against the expected currency depreciation. Similarly, the choice of a strong currency policy requires an adapted wage policy to safeguard the long-term competitive position of the firms. Indeed, with a constant exchange rate and export prices fixed as they are for a small open economy such as Belgium's on the international markets profits are essentially determined by the level of domestic costs and, more specifically, labour costs. When these costs increase more than productivity, profits will be reduced but this cannot go on permanently. After some time a pressure on prices will develop which can be caught in the short and medium term by labour-saving investments; but in the long term market shares will decline. This will lead to higher unemployment, which will increase the budget deficit. Financing this deficit can require an increase in the money supply, but this, for its part, will put pressure on the exchange market.

A third example of the problems that can emerge when policies are not coordinated concerns the existence of a wage indexation scheme in the presence of large external shocks such as an increase in oil prices. A rapid and complete indexation scheme will amplify the shock and this will adversely affect the competitive position when the main partners have different systems linking wages to prices.

These are some examples which illustrate that the choice of a fixed exchange-rate policy not only implies that monetary policy of the leading country needs to be copied relatively well, but also that other economic policies should be adjusted. This alignment should not proceed as far as in the case of monetary policy but the authorities should at least avoid interfering with monetary policy.

Apparently, this conclusion was not drawn by the Belgian policymakers until the early 1980s. Up until 1974 this situation did not create great difficulties since the Belgian economy performed relatively well; the BEF was even a 'strong' currency, at several times eligible for revaluation. To illustrate this, we can refer to the observation that the Belgian short- and long-term interest rates were lower, despite the withholding of tax, than the German ones between, roughly, 1970 and 1973. The non-alignment of the economic policies, other than monetary policy, therefore did not lead to problems. After the first oil crisis, however, the non-alignment of Belgian economic policies led to huge current-account deficits and a weaker currency. This was aggravated by the large monetary financing of the deficit as can be seen in the second column of

Table 7.2 *Budgetary policies, 1975–91*

	Budgetary deficit (percentage of GDP)	Monetary financing of deficit (percentage of total)*
1975	4.7	0.8
1976	5.5	12.2
1977	5.5	9.0
1978	6.0	13.6
1979	7.1	37.2
1980	9.0	39.4
1981	12.6	63.0
1982	11.9	49.4
1983	11.2	26.9
1984	9.1	33.3
1985	8.9	3.7
1986	9.2	18.2
1987	7.3	– 12.4
1988	6.6	0.2
1989	6.5	6.9
1990	5.5	– 13.0
1991	6.3	n.a.

* Sum of borrowing of the Treasury from the central bank and of increases in foreign debt.

Source: European Commission and National Bank of Belgium.

table 7.2. Over the period 1979–82, one-half of the budget deficit was financed by money creation (monetary financing of the deficit is defined as the total of direct and indirect borrowing by the Treasury from the central bank and by foreign borrowing; in this last case foreign exchange is sold directly to the National Bank of Belgium). This money creation was necessary to finance the expensive budgetary policy. The first column of table 7.2 illustrates how rapidly the total budget deficit increased in the second part of the 1970s to attain a maximum value of 12.8 per cent of GDP in 1981. The size of this deficit, by itself, through the effects on the trade balance, put strains on monetary policy. Monetary policy was therefore relatively ambiguous: money creation was expansionary and this had to be offset by a restrictive interest-rate policy. Monetary policy and, more specifically, interest-rate policy had therefore to bear the complete weight of defending the BEF-parity.

Notwithstanding higher interest rates and massive interventions on the exchange market, a devaluation became inevitable. The key explanatory variable was obviously the non-alignment of fiscal policy. The February 1982 devaluation marked the start of a new policy course characterized by an improved, though not perfect, alignment of macroeconomic policies.

Table 7.3 *Official exchange rates of the DEM, in BEF, 1971–1992*

18.12.1971	13.907184
14.2.1973	13.9070
19.3.1973	14.3242
29.6.1973	15.1120
18.10.1976	15.4142
16.10.1978	15.7164
29.9.1979	16.0307
5.10.1981	16.9125
22.2.1982	18.4837
14.6.1982	19.2693
21.3.1983	20.0285
6.4.1986	20.4252
12.1.1987	20.6255

Source: National Bank of Belgium.

Table 7.3 illustrates the nature of the EMS exchange-rate system: it was a system of fixed but adjustable exchange rates. The 1982 devaluation of the Belgian franc amounted to 8.5 per cent. Afterwards, the parity changed a few more times: between mid-1982 and January 1987, the BEF depreciated another 10.38 per cent, mainly as a result of the mid-1982 revaluation of the DEM by more than 4 per cent. Since 1987 the parities have remained constant. These figures illustrate that the BEF had some post-devaluation difficulties.

Note that the devaluation occurred after several years of large current-account deficits and, as noted, monetary financing of the budget deficit. This implied huge exchange-market interventions by the monetary authorities. They amounted to 1058 billion BEF over the period 1977–83 (Annual Report, National Bank of Belgium 1983, 144), being a yearly average of more than 150 billion BEF, or more than 4 per cent of GNP.

Looking further at table 7.3, we arrive at the somewhat cynical conclusion that, as a result of the lack of coordination between the various macroeconomic policies and notwithstanding the strong currency policy, the BEF has lost, *vis-à-vis* the DEM, nearly one-third of its value over the past two decades. This outcome clearly shows that, in the long run, a fixed exchange-rate policy requires that all policy instruments must be directed towards this aim. Leaving this goal to monetary policy alone is asking for trouble, especially when the other instruments are pulling in another direction. Maybe to impose more constraints on other instruments, the National Bank has tied the Belgian Franc more firmly to the DEM since May 1990. The fluctuation margin seems to be 0.5 per cent instead of 2.25 per cent. Of course, this can also be viewed as a 'preparation' for the EMU.

This experience of quasi-fixed or periodic devaluations leads to the question whether the benefits still outweigh the costs of the exchange-rate policy that has been adhered to. It can indeed be questioned if the benefits, linked to the gain in credibility, are indeed observed when the policy is not pursued in a systematic way, i.e. when the exchange rate is not completely fixed. This is not related to monetary policy but to the misalignment of, essentially, fiscal policy. Put differently, is there a credibility gain when the fixed exchange-rate target in reality proves to be only political rhetoric? The point we want to stress is that policy misalignments seriously limit the benefits of the exchange-rate policy. Either fiscal policy will have to be adjusted to the goal of stabilizing exchange rates or the fixed exchange-rate policy will have to be abandoned. In the case of Belgium, the experience of the past two decades shows that, in the end, a devaluation was necessary in order to force policy-makers to adjust the fiscal policy. The experience has been of the kind 'the final test of the cake is in the eating'. This has certainly imposed additional costs on Belgian citizens.

The important role of the EC in the policy change should be stressed. Not only was there, in the late 1970s and early 1980s, a systematic reference to the European average as an illustrator of the bad turn the Belgian economy had taken, but the coordination between policy-makers also helped Belgium to adjust its policies to its real economic possibilities.

Conclusions

The first conclusion that can be drawn from this overview of the Belgian experience is that the theoretically expected results about a fixed exchange-rate system do hold in reality. This policy choice requires monetary policy to target similar values for the same variables (money growth, interest rates, inflation, etc.) as in Germany. Deviations from this rule are only tolerated in the short run which is, furthermore, becoming shorter and shorter. The existence of a dual exchange market created the possibility of prolonging this period slightly, but it does not allow for much additional freedom. Since the dual exchange market has been abolished, this gain in freedom has disappeared. Second, from a European integration point of view, the experience with Belgian monetary policy can be assessed rather positively. Together with Germany and The Netherlands, Belgium has systematically aimed for fixed exchange rates within the Community. In this regard it was made clear – although we can regret that the coordination process was not intense enough to avoid the problem altogether – that, given the objective of stabilizing the DEM exchange rate, wage and fiscal policy were completely misaligned. Notwithstanding the clear amelioration, budgetary policy is still a threat to monetary policy: the policy alignment is not yet fully complete. The large deficit and the high debt-income ratio still create a permanent danger of a resort to monetary finance. A credible monetary policy, therefore, requires a credible fiscal policy which is not only directed at reducing the deficit but also at the debt-income ratio. The lessons from this experience are clear: a small country has to keep as close as possible to the policy objectives of its economically and financially dominant neighbour. Since the policy adjustments have gone further by the announced strengthened link with the DEM, even less divergence from the German situation will be allowed. This will put more strain on economic policy. We must hope that the third step in the integration process, more intensive policy coordination, will overcome this. It should be clear to the authorities that even more rigour will be required in the application of the conclusions drawn from the 'strong currency goal'. Put more positively, we can state that a higher degree of policy coordination within the EC can be very important for Belgium since this could be a 'cheaper' way to build up credibility than by doing it through persuing convincing macroeconomic policies. This, however, implies an additional loss of autonomy, especially with respect to fiscal policy.

References

Giavazzi F., S. Micossi and M. Miller (1988) *The European Monetary System*, Cambridge, Cambridge University Press.

National Bank of Belgium, *Annual Reports*.

PART II: FOREIGN RELATIONS

Chapter 8

External trade policy

Michèle Konings and M.A.G. van Meerhaeghe

---

1. TRADE – *Michèle Konings*

It is not easy to draw up a balance of the advantages and disadvantages of the European integration concerning external trade for Belgium, or rather for the BLEU (Belgian–Luxemburgian Economic Union). Indeed, there is no systematic study devoted to this subject.[1] On the other hand, it seems very difficult to trace the role of the Common Market in the development of the external position of Belgium, as far as this factor interacts with several other elements, such as the measures of the national economic policy and the structural changes of the international environment – especially on the level of the international division of labour or also external events such as the oil crises or the variations in the rate of exchange.

Moreover, the entry of Belgium and Luxemburg into the EEC has never raised any controversies which was the case for some other countries, so that the need to compare the costs and advantages of the integration seemed not as evident as elsewhere. The integration of Belgium in a vast economic area is all the more interesting since a great part of its economy is based on external trade.

In the first part of this chapter we look at the characteristics of Belgium as a small, open economy. We will try to analyse the effects of the integration on the external trade of the BLEU in a second part. The third part of this chapter will look into the specific elements of the external trade of the BLEU especially in terms of its geographical distribution, the composition per product or branch of activity, and examine these points more closely in accordance with the effects of participation of the BLEU in the Community.

A small, open economy

Despite its size, Belgium plays a considerable part in world trade.

Table 8.1 *Shares of the external flows of exchange in the GDP, 1960–93*

Years	Exportations of goods and services at current prices (in % of GDP)		Importations of goods and services at current prices (in % of GDP)	
	Belgium	EUR	Belgium	EUR
1960	39.9	19.6	40.8	19.0
1961	41.2	19.0	42.1	18.4
1962	42.8	18.4	43.0	18.3
1963	44.0	18.3	45.2	18.6
1964	44.9	18.5	45.3	18.9
1965	44.3	18.8	44.5	18.9
1966	46.1	19.2	46.9	19.0
1967	45.1	19.2	44.7	18.7
1968	47.3	20.2	47.0	19.5
1969	51.5	21.0	50.4	20.5
1970	53.9	21.7	51.3	21.2
1971	52.5	22.0	50.2	21.1
1972	53.1	22.0	49.4	21.0
1973	57.8	23.2	55.4	22.9
1974	63.7	27.0	63.0	27.7
1975	55.8	25.0	55.3	24.6
1976	58.7	26.4	58.2	26.7
1977	57.6	26.8	58.2	26.3
1978	55.6	26.2	56.3	25.0
1979	60.8	26.9	62.6	26.8
1980	62.9	27.2	65.4	28.1
1981	68.2	28.6	69.8	28.7
1982	71.8	28.6	72.9	28.5
1983	74.7	28.7	72.9	28.0
1984	79.1	30.5	77.4	29.6
1985	76.9	30.9	74.4	29.5
1986	70.7	27.9	66.7	25.7
1987	69.3	27.2	66.2	25.7
1988	72.6	27.1	68.9	26.2
1989	76.7	28.5	73.3	27.8
1990	74.2	28.3	71.1	27.3
1991	74.4	28.6	71.3	27.1
1992	75.1	29.1	72.0	27.5
1993	76.3	29.6	73.0	27.9

Source: Commission of the European Communities, Directorate – General for Economic and Financial Affairs, Current Balance, relative growth, competitiveness, exchange rates and interest rates – Tables, January 1992.

According to GATT (1990, table 11) the BLEU is at position ten of the table in order of importance of exportation and importation in value, with respective parts of 3.2 per cent and 3.1 per cent of the world flows in 1989. In 1990, Belgium gained one place in the table of the world's best exporting countries, going from tenth to ninth position. Within the EEC the BLEU reaches sixth position for imports (with 8.6 per cent in 1990) and sixth position for exports (with 8.7 per cent), according to statistics from Eurostat (1991).

A first measure of the opening of an economy consists of examining the importance of exports and imports in proportion to the GDP (Table 8.1). At the time of the establishment of the Common Market, the export and import rates were particularly high for Belgium, and superior to the average rates of the member countries. During the following three decades, the share of the external trade (exports and imports) in the GDP has not ceased to increase: from 40 per cent in 1960, it went up to 50 per cent in 1970, to more than 60 per cent in 1980, and in 1990 it reached more than 70 per cent for imports and almost 75 per cent for exports. During the same period, the average rates for the Community also increased, all staying below those of Belgium. The difference became even more marked: in 1960, the ratio between the share of exports (or imports) in the GDP of Belgium and the corresponding part for the EEC was 2.0 per cent; in 1990 it became 2.5 per cent.

From the analysis of this and other indicators (CEE 1985, Konings 1986), it can be concluded that the characteristics of the small, open economy of Belgium are very distinctive, even compared to the countries of comparable size, with consequently all the advantages and disadvantages. On the one hand, the country profits more from favourable conditions of the international environment, the external trade having a key role in the economy. On the other hand, the country is more vulnerable for conjunctural movements coming from outside and thus being independent from the possible actions of the national authorities. This also implies a particular interest for joined actions and the harmonization of policies with the partner Countries.

The effects of European integration on external trade

Trade development after the Common Market

It is not an easy task to point out the positive and negative effects of European integration since the development of trade depends on various factors of which it is difficult to estimate the importance. Before presenting a short survey of the studies on this subject, it may be useful to sketch the development of the external trade of the BLEU in broad outline. Table 8.2 presents comparative data for the BLEU and the EEC for the period 1958–90.

Table 8.2 *External trade and trade balance of the BLEU and the EEC(12), 1958–90*

	Exports		Imports		Trade balance	
Year	BLEU	EEC(12)	BLEU	EEC(12)	BLEU	EEC(12)
			Value in millions of ECU			
1958	3.052	34.667	3.136	37.249	− 84	− 2.582
1959	3.298	37.645	3.445	39.468	− 147	− 1.823
1960	3.775	43.233	3.957	46.711	− 182	− 3.478
1961	3.924	46.354	4.219	49.540	− 295	− 3.186
1962	4.324	48.737	4.555	54.079	− 231	− 5.342
1963	4.839	53.277	5.112	60.287	− 273	− 7.010
1964	5.590	59.827	5.922	68.351	− 332	− 8.524
1965	6.382	66.400	6.374	74.040	− 8	− 7.640
1966	6.829	72.690	7.174	80.180	− 345	− 7.490
1967	7.032	76.358	7.176	82.700	− 144	− 6.342
1968	8.164	85.847	8.333	91.463	− 169	− 5.616
1969	10.065	100.447	9.989	107.893	+ 76	− 7.446
1970	11.609	116.157	11.362	124.371	+ 247	− 8.214
1971	12.184	129.381	12.357	134.474	− 173	− 5.093
1972	14.404	143.048	13.812	147.481	+ 592	− 4.433
1973	18.203	177.549	17.910	187.659	+ 293	− 10.110
1974	23.703	240.814	25.015	266.901	− 1.312	− 26.087
1975	23.193	249.184	24.818	263.229	− 1.625	− 14.045
1976	29.340	304.379	31.714	333.353	− 2.374	− 28.974
1977	32.892	345.947	35.418	365.822	− 2.526	− 19.875
1978	35.203	374.530	38.093	387.096	− 2.890	− 12.566
1979	41.033	437.602	44.053	469.963	− 3.020	− 32.361
1980	46.459	497.137	51.612	557.746	− 5.153	− 60.609
1981	49.881	571.054	55.613	618.870	− 5.732	− 47.816
1982	53.551	626.652	59.095	672.187	− 5.544	− 45.535
1983	58.460	671.884	62.475	707.694	− 4.015	− 35.810
1984	65.956	776.772	70.750	809.357	− 4.794	− 32.585
1985	70.649	849.936	74.347	874.675	− 3.698	− 24.739
1986	70.168	806.958	70.401	796.005	− 233	+ 10.953
1987	71.952	829.911	72.605	829.135	− 653	+ 776
1988	77.854	906.730	80.738	930.594	− 2.884	− 23.864
1989	90.851	1.043.289	93.008	1.073.552	− 2.157	− 30.263
1990	92.962	1.081.428	98.571	1.129.055	− 5.609	− 47.627
			Average yearly variation in %			
1970/1960	11.9	10.4	11.1	10.3		
1980/1970	14.9	15.6	16.3	16.2		
1990/1980	7.2	8.1	6.7	7.3		

Source: Eurostat (1988) '*Commerce Extérieur Annuaire Statistique*', Thème 6, Série A et Eurostat (1991), *Commerce Extérieur Annuaire Statistique*, Rétrospective 1958–1990, Thème 6, Série A.

The average variation rates calculated over periods of ten years show that the growth of the flows of the BLEU has been very close to that of the Community. During the 1960s, it became nevertheless a little faster, while over recent years it has been weaker. This is reflected in the share of the BLEU in all the exports and imports of the EEC. For exports, the share has grown from 8.7 per cent in 1960 to 10 per cent in 1970; it then diminished to 9.3 per cent in 1980 and 8.6 per cent in 1990. As for imports, the upward movement continued: the share has increased from 8.5 per cent in 1960 to 9.1 per cent in 1970 and 9.3 per cent in 1980, subsequently decreasing to 8.7 per cent in 1990.

During the 1970s, the external position of the BLEU deteriorated (table 8.2). The first oil crisis was not solely responsible for the degradation of the trade balance; indeed, the external competitiveness of the manufacturing industry has also severely diminished which resulted in a loss of 2 per cent of the market share between 1975–6 and 1980–1 (OECD 1986: 20). These problems are mentioned in the third part of this chapter.

Facing this development, in 1982 the government decided to devalue the Belgian franc, and took other measures to restrain the inflationary effects and to restore the competitiveness of firms. Indeed, in 1983, the external deficit diminished by 1,529 million ECU; but nevertheless the trade balance remained until the end of 1985, mainly affected by the oil bill. The fall of the price of oil and the depreciation of the dollar in 1986 had a strong positive influence, though it did not last (see table 8.2).

Estimations of the effects on external EC trade

During the years which followed the establishment of the Common Market, an extensive literature has developed, dealing with the effects of European integration on the exchanges. This is not the place to go into the methodology used, but we can say that most of the studies are based either on a 'residual' approach, which consists of calculating the differences between observed flows and hypothetical flows which correspond to a situation of non-integration, the so-called 'anti-world', or on an analytical approach based on the construction of explanatory models of external trade, in which economic integration intervenes as explanatory variable.

Each method is naturally subject to criticism; and since international transactions depend on a great number of factors, it is difficult to isolate the effects of one variable concerning economic integration. Moreover, many studies contain rather strong hypotheses especially concerning the 'anti-world', in the case of the residual approach which implies without doubt important systematic faults. It is dangerous to estimate the development of external trade flows of the BLEU, which would have been produced if the Common Market had not been created, and consequently the comparison with the flows actually observed appears to be delicate. Nevertheless, the analysis of all the different studies can give us some conclusions about the direction of the effects and the range of the results.

- according to the methods used, the results present considerable differences, particularly concerning the extension of the impact;
- it seems nevertheless that in most of the studies, the net effect obtained at the end of the period is positive and in conformity with the process on the basis of the theory of the customs unions;
- in the case of the BLEU, the impact seems weaker than in the large countries;
- the reasons quoted are relative to the initial level of the tariffs before the harmonization, to the effect of the demotivation of the intra-Benelux exchanges and to the influence of the size of the markets.

Finally, it is without doubt regrettable that no research has recently been devoted to a study of the impact of the EEC over a long period.

Detailed analysis

The influence of European integration on the external exchanges of the BLEU can also be shown clearly by the study of certain specific aspects concerning the geographical distribution and the composition per branch of activity of the flows. First, for the geographical distribution of the exchanges, the dependence of the BLEU towards the member countries of the EEC should be strongly emphasized. Before the creation of the Common Market, the share of exchanges with the European countries was already predominant, which is explained by the facilities which offer vicinity, low transport costs, similar consumer behaviour in the neighbouring countries and market accessibility. Exports to wider destinations which involve high costs and risks have represented only a residual part of the external trade of the BLEU.

The concentration of the external flows increased between 1960 and 1990 (Table 8.3). Nevertheless, the increase took place mainly during the 1960s. During the 1970s, the radical changes of the international environment (oil crises, the rise of newly industrialized countries) caused a certain decrease in the intra-EEC trade (except for imports over the last few years). The concentration is particularly strong within the three neighbouring countries of France, Germany and The Netherlands. The cumulative part of these countries in the exchanges of the BLEU increased during the 1960s (from 42.9 per cent to 63.4 per cent for exports between 1958 and 1970 and from 44.4 per cent to 55.1 per cent for imports). Following the oil crises and the movements which have affected the international division of labour, this cumulative part has

Table 8.3 *Importance of the intra-EEC trade, 1960–90*

Years	Share of the intra-EEC trade in the total trade of the BLEU (in %) Exports	Imports
1960	60.7	56.6
1970	75.2	66.3
1980	73.2	61.6
1990	75.1	70.7

Source: Eurostat (1988) 'Commerce Extérieur, Annuaire Statistique', Thème 6, Série A et Eurostat (1991) *Commerce Extérieur, Annuaire Statistique*, Rétrospective 1958–1990, Thème 6, Série A.

decreased slightly as a result, but in 1991 it increased to 50 per cent. France and Germany in particular have increased their importance in the exchanges with the BLEU, while The Netherlands, once a privileged partner in the Benelux, faced a relative decline in its bilateral trade with Belgium (see Table 8.4).

Table 8.4 *Relative importance of the exchanges of the BLEU with the three main partners, 1958–91*

Year	Share in % of the total exchanges of the BLEU					
	Exports			Imports		
	France	Germany	Netherlands	France	Germany	Netherlands
1958	10.6	11.6	20.7	11.6	17.1	15.7
1960	10.4	15.8	21.3	13.6	17.0	14.8
1970	19.9	24.1	19.4	17.1	23.4	14.6
1980	19.4	21.2	15.2	14.4	19.7	16.4
1980	19.4	21.2	15.2	14.4	19.7	16.4
1991	19.1	23.7	13.7	15.8	23.5	17.2

Source: Ministère des Affaires Economiques, DGED, *L'Economie belge en . . ., Rapport Annuel*, Bruxelles.

The effects of the enlargement of the EEC can also be pointed out. In 1972, the United Kingdom's share in the external trade of the BLEU was 4.4 per cent for exports and 6.4 per cent for imports. In 1980, these shares became respectively 8.5 per cent and 8.1 per cent and in 1991 8.7 per cent and 8.3 per cent.

The openness of the EEC towards the Iberian market also had an accelerating effect on the exchanges with this region. For exports of the BLEU, in 1985 Spain represented 1.0 per cent of the total and Portugal 0.3 per cent. In 1991, these rates were 2.3 per cent and 0.7 per cent. For imports of the BLEU, the effect was less spectacular; Spain's share has increased from 1.1 per cent to 1.3 per cent between 1985 and 1991 and Portugal's share has remained stable. These developments are situated in a more general view of the progression of the sales of the member countries of the EEC towards the Iberian peninsula, a movement which results in the combination of the opening of the borders with the need to respond to the internal needs of development of this region. As for the structures of the exchanges per product, some studies have pointed out that these are responsible for the deficiencies in the external performance of the BLEU, both for the criteria related to the conditions of the offer and to the development of the demand.

As for the aspects involving supply, Belgium's specialization is based particularly on capital- and natural resources-intensive products, at least as far as trade with the other developed countries is concerned, although the position of the country is weak in qualified work-intensive products (see the studies of Culem (1984) and Tharakan and Waelbroeck 1988).

If the products are classified according to their content and technology, it seems that compared with the average of the OECD countries, the share of the sectors with low technology is higher for the exports of the BLEU and the share of the sectors with high technology is, on the contrary, weaker (OECD 1986). Belgium's performances are average even compared to other small countries equally put at a disadvantage by their size for investment in R&D. It seems that the heritage of the industrial past but also the orientation of industrial policy are responsible for the importance of the traditional industries to the disadvantage of the sectors with a technological superiority. Moreover during the period from the 1970s to the early 1980s this less-favourable orientation hardly changed.

Moreover, a comparison of the sectorial specialization of the BLEU with the development of world demand per category of products also indicates deficiencies. Studies of the EEC (1985) on competitiveness as well as those of the Planning Bureau (Bernard and Roosens 1987 and 1988) show that the problems of Belgian industry came particularly from the incompetence of firms to develop themselves towards the productions for which the progression of the external demand is dynamic. The importance of the sectors of low demand is too high.

So in 1986, the share of products of low demand in all the BLEU exports was 41 per cent against 27 per cent for the EEC (8), 15 per cent for the USA and 16 per cent for Japan (Bernard and Roosens 1988). For the BLEU, the share of the products of high demand was only 23 per cent and that of the products with average demand 35 per cent. Moreover, if we look at the development since the beginning of the 1970s, it seems that the BLEU, like the other members of the EEC, has despecialized in the exports of the most-demanded products. In fact, a comparison can be made with the classification of the products according to their technological level: the products for which world demand is increasing are generally those of high technology.

These deficiencies partly explain the loss of market shares noted by the BLEU. The OECD (1986) made an analysis of 'constant market shares' which studied the difference of the growth rate of Belgian exports and world imports (external demand) of manufactured products. It distinguished three effects of which the first has to do with the geographical distribution of exports, the second concerns the range of products and the third the residual effect which can be interpreted as competitiveness. It seems that this residual effect has always been negative and important since the mid-1960s.

Another characteristic aspect of the external exchanges of the BLEU is the importance of intra-branch trade. Referring to the studies of Grubel (1970), this type of exchange is defined as 'the phenomenon that countries often export and import simultaneously products which are perfect substitutes except for differences in the products' location or timing of manufacture'.[2] The interest for this type of exchange has been raised by the development of important commercial flows between developed countries, leaning on similar products belonging to the same industry and which are consequently no result of the differences in the comparative advantages of the partner countries.

The existence of these flows are partly explained by the elements relative to supply and partly by elements relative to demand. It needs to be said that the exchanged products are not completely identical. They are indeed 'differentiated', either in a horizontal manner (according to the combination of the characteristics of the products), or in a vertical manner (according to the quality of the product), or in a technological way (on the basis of different techniques).

In other words, the differentiated products correspond to the diversity of consumer preferences to satisfy the same need. The intra-industrial trade consequently has more chance to bring about and to develop between countries of which the conditions of the offer and the structure of the demand are comparable. So, the integration of the European countries in an economic union is a stimulating factor for the development of this type of trade. This is especially true for small countries which are very dependent on their neighbours, which is the case for Belgium.

Different indicators permit the measurement of the importance of this type of trade. A comparative study for the period 1970–80 (Konings 1986) shows that the importance of the intra-branch trade has increased in all the EEC countries and that Belgium is situated among the countries which have the strongest intra-branch specialization.

Conclusion

Without expressing an opinion on the influence of European integration on the external trade of the BLEU, keeping in mind the difficulty of putting this element aside from so many others, it may nevertheless be useful to highlight some positive and negative aspects. From a positive side, it is certain that the abolition of the borders for the exchanges is a stimulating factor in the sense that economic interpenetration of the countries contributes to the acceleration of economic growth. In the case of the BLEU, as has been shown above, because of its high degree of openness, exports play an even more fundamental role than in the other countries as the driving force for growth.

Many studies carried out during the years which followed the establishment of the Common Market, tend to show that the BLEU has profited by the expected effect of creating exchanges with the partner countries, although without doubt to a lesser degree than the large countries. The explanation of these weaker results are the low initial level of tariffs of the BLEU, the diversion of trade which was produced to the disadvantage of the BENELUX, and the effects caused by the size of the countries. On the other hand, it can also be observed that since the 1970s, the BLEU has known certain less-favourable developments although they cannot be attributed to a 'Common Market' effect. It seems that Belgium shows a deterioration of its competitiveness which is noticeable by a loss of market shares. The structure of exports per product presents deficiencies: the importance of the heavy industries of which the demand only slowly develops, is too high.

Moreover, in terms of 'comparative advantages', it seems that Belgium has diminished its specialization not only for products of low technology but unfortunately also for products of high technology to the benefit of average products, relatively standardized.

Finally, as for the geographical distribution, we have noted a strong concentration of exchanges on the European markets and most particularly on the three neighbouring countries. This concentration presents advantages particularly in terms of costs and facilities, but also inconveniences. A more flexible and diversified structure allows more profits from new markets with perspectives.

Notes

1 This comparison was made by M. Herman in the report 'L'achèvement du marché intérieur de la Communauté européenne' presented before the Chamber of Representatives. Ref. 20–850/2–86/87, session 1986–1987, 10 October 1987. (Second part: La Belgique et le marché intérieur européen — Leçons du passé.)

2 Grubel, N. (1970) 'The theory of intra-industry trade, published by I.A. Mac Dougall and R.A. Snape: *Studies in International Economics*, Amsterdam, North-Holland, 36.

References

Bernard, P. and R. Roosens, (1987) 'Performances comparées de la Belgique à l'exportation des produits de l'industrie manufacturière (1972–1985)', *Planning Papers*, Bureau du Plan, Brussels, July.

Bernard, P. and R. Roosens, (1988) 'Analyse de l'évolution comparée des structures des exportations, de la production et de la demande intérieure ainsi que des résultats commerciaux extérieurs de l'industrie manufacturière de dix pays très industrialisés', Bureau du Plan, Brussels, July.

CEE (1985) 'La Compétitivité de l'Industrie européenne, un bilan et Les Déterminants de l'Offre industrielle communautaire', *Economie Européenne*, no. 25, chaps. 1 and 2, September.

Commission of the European Communities, Directorate General for Economic and Financial Affairs, 1992, Current Balance, relative growth, competitiveness, exchange rates and interest rates – Tables, January.

Culem, C. (1984) 'Comparative advantage and industrial restructuring. The Belgian case 1970–1980', *Cahiers Economiques de Bruxelles*, no. 103, third quarter.

Eurostat (1988) 'Commerce extérieur – annuaire statistique', thème 6, series A.

Eurostat (1991) 'Commerce extérieur – statistiques mensuelles', thème 6, series B, no. 4.

GATT (1990) *Le Commerce International 89–90*, vol. I, Geneva.

Konings, M. (1986) 'Evaluation des performances de la Belgique face à la spécialisation internationale', *Aperçu Economique Trimestriel*, no. 3/86, 51–105.

Lafay, G. (1974) 'Spécialisation internationale et croissance nationale. Une approche par la Théorie des Créneaux', *Revue Economique*, vol. 25, no. 3, May, 395–435.

Lafay, G. (1976) 'Compétitivité, Spécialisation et Demande Mondiale, *Economie et Statistique*, no. 80, July–August, 25–6.

OECD (1986) 'Belgique–Luxembourg', *Etudes Economiques*, 1985/1986, Paris, August.

Tharakan, P.K.M. and J. Waelbroeck (1988) 'Has human capital become a scarce factor in Belgium?', *Cahiers Economiques de Bruxelles*, no. 118, second quarter.

2. POLICY – *M.A.G. van Meerhaeghe*

In order to help understand the last section related to Belgium, we indicate first the extent to which the Community has taken over former national powers.

Principles

Since the Common Market applies to goods imported from outside the Community (Article 9,*2*), a common commercial policy (CCP) towards non-EC countries is essential. Hence, Article 3,*b* which provides for the establishment of a common customs tariff and of a CCP towards third countries. The CCP is closely linked to the internal market.

However, the Commission's and the Council's policy freedom is restricted: they have to respect a number of aims expressed in the Treaty. In the preamble to the Treaty the Member States underline their desire 'to contribute, by means of a common commercial policy, to the progressive abolition of restrictions on international trade'. The readiness to contribute to the development of international trade and the lowering of barriers to trade is conditional upon 'reciprocity and mutual advantage' (Article 18). On the other hand, Article 18 refers only to customs duties.

The contents of the common policy could hardly be foreseen and was therefore not laid down in the Treaty. Only one general and debatable consideration is put forward: account is to be taken of the likelihood that the abolition of customs duties between Member States will make firms in the EC more competitive (Article 110, second paragraph). According to the Commission the removal of obstacles to the growth of world trade should therefore not be feared.

Article 113,*1* gives examples of a common commercial policy: tariff rates, the conclusion of tariff and trade agreements, the achievement of uniformity in measures of liberalization, export policy, anti-dumping and countervailing duties. It states that the CCP should be based on uniform principles, but it does not define that policy.

Since the exclusive powers of the Community – member countries may not enter into international agreements on their own – are not described, Member States sometimes believe that these powers are exceeded and they want their point of view to be considered. Hence the differing interpretations by Commission and Council. According to the Council the CCP tries to influence the volume or flow of trade. According to the broader view of the Commission it includes all measures relating to international trade (even tariffs and regulations on customs matters).

In fact, the Council plays a decisive role (Article 113,*2*,*3* and *4*). The Commission is in charge of the common customs administration and conducts 'negotiations in consultation with a special committee appointed by the Council to assist the Commission in this task and within the framework of such directives as the Council may issue to it' (Article 113,*3*). The special committee is referred to as the 'mother-in-law committee'.

National restrictions on third-country imports imply control of the imports of the same goods from member countries (given the free movement within the Community and the differential access to the Common Market for these goods). They can be authorized by Article 115.

According to the Court of Justice (International Rubber Agreement Opinion, 4 October 1979) the Treaty preference for international trade liberalization does not preclude an international trade policy aiming at more trade regulation for certain products. This pragmatic point of view has allowed the introduction of voluntary export restraints and orderly market agreements.

Implementation

The foreign-trade structure and the significance of foreign trade in the member countries' economies are very different. This reveals itself in the widespread, but uneven appeal to Article 115. The Benelux countries do not apply this Article (the BLEU and The Netherlands have already formed a customs union at the establishment of the EC: see chapter 3).

Whereas it is difficult to separate external trade policy from foreign policy, foreign policy remains the responsibility of the Member States, notwithstanding an embryo of European political cooperation. Hence, it is not surprising that in the field of the CCP the Commission receives its instructions from the Member States. Its decisions are intergovernmental rather than supranational. However, the European Union Treaty signed at Maastricht on 7 February 1992 provides for a common foreign and security policy (Title V).

Although the Council can act by qualified majority, it tries to reach a consensus – which is not easy, given the fundamental opposition between a group of member countries in favour of a more protectionist position and another group preferring a free-trade policy. The CCP is anything but common (e.g. Article 115, state trading).

Reciprocity

Not only the Community producers, but also third-country exporters will benefit from an internal market of 320 million consumers, with uniform norms and administrative procedures. Some member countries, such as France, argue that the main beneficiaries of the single market will be Japanese and American companies and that third countries should be obliged to 'pay' for that advantage.

According to those mostly southern European member countries, reciprocity means identical treatment. For example, subsidiaries of foreign banks, already established in the Community, should be denied the right of pan-European operations, unless reciprocity is granted in their home market. After setting up assembly plants in a Member State which is liberal towards foreign investment, third-country firms should not have access from within to other Member States. This point of view was not shared by the majority of the member countries.

On 19 October 1988 the Commission reserved 'the right to make access to the benefits of 1992 for non-member countries' firms conditional upon a guarantee of similar opportunities – or at least non-discriminatory opportunities – in those firms' own countries'. Reciprocity does not mean 'that all partners must make the same concessions', nor that the Community will ask its partners to adopt legislation identical to its own (e.g. the US interstate banking laws which limit the geographical and operating freedom on their home territory). For tests and certification, the Community will negotiate mutual recognition agreements where needed.

Liberation of trade in services towards third countries is to be negotiated, on the basis of reciprocity, in the Uruguay Round. The same applies to government procurement. The free-trade position of the Community was adopted after heavy external pressure and notwithstanding the strong opposition of the Southern European countries.

Belgium's position

As an open economy Belgium is in favour of free trade and in this respect its objectives coincide in theory with those of the Community. A stable relationship with our main trading partners is an advantage. The position of Antwerp, one of the most important ports of Western Europe, is strengthened by free trade and improved relations with its large hinterland.

From the above analysis it appears that the extensive and exclusive Community powers in the field of external trade has 'bereft' Belgium of similar powers. Moreover, the implications of the common agricultural policy impair the export possibilities of third countries which thus cannot earn the foreign exchange necessary to import from the Community (and from Belgium). Belgian firms have suffered from retaliation by the United States in connection with the CCP.

In the framework of the Benelux union Belgium has been accustomed since 1956 to the 'collective' conclusion of trade agreements. It is impossible to compare this with hypothetical national agreements which would have been concluded, if the Benelux or the EC had not existed.

But normally the bargaining power of the Benelux union and especially of the EC is higher than that of Belgium. On the other hand, in collective negotiations it is impossible to take into account every interest of every country.

'Reciprocity' is less an issue for Belgium since it has only a few 'national champions' and many important economic decision-centres are situated abroad (cf. chapter 3).

The main advantage of the CCP is the larger bargaining power of the EC. However, it is impossible to prove whether it equals or differs from the disadvantages resulting from a CCP which leaves much to be desired and does not necessarily look after Belgium's interests. A similar conclusion was drawn in Part 1 of this chapter in respect of the influence of the European integration on Belgian external trade.

Reference

Meerhaeghe, M.A.G. van (1992) *International Economic Institutions* (6th edn.), Dordrecht, Boston, London, Kluwer Academic Publishers, chapter 8.

Chapter 9

Foreign policy cooperation and security policy

Alfred Cahen

In order to make progress, the European movement has had to follow paths which its 'founding fathers' did not necessarily envisage when they laid its foundations, in particular the Paris Treaty establishing the ECSC.

The purpose of the enterprise was essentially political, the aim being that it should develop into a European Union not only with economic responsibilities, but also with responsibility in both the foreign policy and security fields — see the Preamble to the Paris Treaty and the positions adopted by some of the 'founding fathers' such as Paul-Henri Spaak (1969: 99–100).

In large part, the project in question almost came to fruition with the European Defence Community and its logical corollary, the European Political Community.

The failure of these enterprises prompted the Six to re-launch the process of European construction with the Rome Treaties. The fact that the advocates of these Treaties had been obliged to confine themselves essentially to the economic aspects of European integration did not in any way change what they believed was the overall political vocation of their undertaking.

That said, circumstances dictated that if the movement to build Europe was to acquire its foreign policy and security dimensions it would have to follow paths other than the Community one, namely European Political Confederation (EPC) and Western European Union (WEU).

But it must be emphasized that whereas EPC and WEU did not, strictly speaking, come within the Community framework, they do, by virtue of the express will of their Member States, come within the Communities' sphere of influence (see the Luxembourg or Davignon Report of 23 October 1970 and the document on a European identity published in Copenhagen on 14 December 1973 by the Nine and the Platform on European security interests adopted by the Seven on 27 October 1987).

Obviously, the nature of the Communities and that of EPC and WEU (and in the latter's case its composition) are different, as indeed have been their respective developments.

Be that as it may, EPC and indeed WEU have to be considered, alongside the Communities, as elements in the process of European construction.

Accordingly, it is entirely justified to assess the costs and benefits for the individual member States of their participation in EPC and in WEU on the same basis as the costs of, and benefits from, their membership of the Communities.

European political cooperation

EPC gives the process of European construction a 'foreign policy dimension'.

It is still too early to speak of a European foreign policy. That is still some way off, the main reasons being that:

- the powers of the EPC in this field are not exclusive since its Member States retain — in addition to EPC commitments — almost complete control over their national diplomacy;
- the obligations to which its Member States subscribe within the EEC are restricted to those important, but nevertheless limited, ones which are articulated in Article 30 of The Single European Act.

It is nevertheless true that the progress made by EPC over nearly 20 years has been such that its members have felt increasingly obliged to confer together ('a concertation reflex' (Copenhagen Report — 14 December 1973)) and that political cooperation has persuaded the participant states to adopt public positions on many international problems. They make declarations; they make démarches and make them public; they vote together in the United Nations and explain their reasons to each other; they act by common consent at international conferences. By dint of repetition and reaffirmation, these stances gradually came to represent a political line from which the participants would find it hard to deviate. The credibility of each country on the international stage does in fact exact a certain degree of cohesion in the positions they adopt (Schoutheete: 161).

It is difficult to define the cost of Political Cooperation since it is so small, whether in terms of the abandonment of sovereignty (see above) or in administrative costs, since its Secretariat is particularly light in structure.

On the other hand, its progress has brought with it a proliferation of meetings at ministerial level, at the level of its Political Committee and expert groups, and also a growing interest on the part of national administrations. For the latter, therefore, there is a 'work cost' which will increase.

But in the opinion of all its protagonists, the benefits are considerable (also for Belgium) and they can be grouped under the following headings:

(a) *exchange of information* which ensures that the information gathered by any one member of EPC is made available to the others;

(b) *diplomatic weight*. The diplomatic weight of each of the participant States is in a way enhanced by that of its partners, particularly in the case of a small country like Belgium.

Two examples may illustrate this:

- the Conference on Cooperation and Security in Europe. This is a field in which EPC has been active since its inception and which is undeniably one of its successes. There is no doubt that the essential part that its members have played and are continuing to play with regard to this Conference is due to the remarkable cohesion they have shown and which is out of all proportion with the rôle that any one of them, even the most influential, could have played alone;
- the Arab-Israeli problem: the Venice Declaration of June 1980 would not have had the impact it did have if it had been issued by one of the Nine and not by the then Nine collectively;

(c) *the external image*. EPC has succeeded in creating a kind of external image of European diplomacy which benefits each of the participant States.

The reality of this image is felt for example in:

- the United Nations where – although the votes of the Twelve are often far from being convergent – third countries are increasingly looking for contact with the Twelve as a whole;
- relations with the Arab League (Euro-Arab dialogue);
- relations with the Association of South-East Asian Nations (ASEAN);
- relations with the Andean Pact countries;
- relations with the Group of Central American States and with the Contadora.

(d) *mutual support*. Belgium also benefits from the fact that, as a result of developments in Political Cooperation, its partners refrain, at the very least, from thwarting the diplomatic activity of EPC and at best – and this is what is happening most often – give it their support.

Example: the Falklands Affair (1982)

Fight against terrorism

At its meeting in Rome in December 1975, the European Council decided that the Ministers of the Interior would henceforward meet to discuss questions coming within their competence, particularly in the field of public order.

The first meeting of these Interior Ministers took place in Luxembourg on 29 June 1976. They agreed on the need for joint action to step up the fight against organized international crime and more particularly against terrorism. Since then, Ministers have met frequently. They have at their disposal a group of senior officials from the Interior Ministries which, in a way, constitute a Political Committee, and also working groups, all of them being referred to as 'Trevi Groups' after the name of the Roman fountain.

This work is marked by understandable discretion. The meetings provide an opportunity for Ministers and specialists to exchange technical information and experience and they also provide mutual practical support.

The *cost* of this is minimal since, once again, there has been no abandonment of sovereignty, nor is there any administrative expenditure.

The *benefit* is difficult to assess on account of the discretion surrounding the work and its results, but the specialists involved maintain that it helps to bring an increased level of effectiveness within the Twelve in the fight against terrorism.

Missing: legal cooperation

Despite the efforts made since 1976 (for example, draft convention on the compulsory judgement or extradition of those responsible for hostage-taking, the proposal for a European judicial area, the plan to establish a European criminal court competent to try those responsible for attacks or organized crime, draft multilateral extradition agreement) it has not been possible so far to establish any definite legal cooperation between what were the Nine, then the Ten and finally the Twelve.

Nevertheless, the Solemn Declaration in Stuttgart in June 1983 contained a chapter dealing with the harmonization of legislation and efforts are still continuing, particularly within the framework of the meetings of Justice Ministers and their senior officials.

With no tangible progress having been made so far, this failure could prove to be extremely costly as the movement for freedom of circulation, freedom of establishment and increased trade gathers momentum with the approach of the internal market (1 January 1993).

Security

Europe of the Twelve does not have a 'security dimension'. That said, there has been no lack of effort to create one.[1]

Yet there is an institution which has always seemed to have the vocation to become the centre out of which a European security dimension could develop, i.e. European Political Cooperation. Any foreign policy without a security component is incomplete and consequently unbalanced. It therefore seemed natural that Political Cooperation should extend its action in this direction. During the 1980s, major initiatives have been launched by several member States aimed at formally endowing Political Cooperation with significant responsibilities for security matters. But these initiatives have met with only partial success. At present, Political Cooperation is competent to deal with the economic and political aspects of security but not with security as such and in its entirety.

Article 30, paragraph 6 (a) of the Single European Act – the latest statement on the matter – is clear on this point.

Why have these initiatives been only a partial success? In essence, because three of the then Ten members of the European Community – Denmark, Greece and Ireland – could not unreservedly accept a complete European security dimension. The Seven others therefore decided to create this dimension themselves and, accordingly, to reactivate an organization which was at their disposal but which had not been used for the past ten years: Western European Union.

However, in the field of security for which it is competent, WEU has even less exclusive responsibility than Political Cooperation has with regard to international relations.

First, with the exception of their commitments to the Atlantic Alliance, its member States retain full sovereignty in defence matters. Second, the number of bilateral cooperation arrangements is increasing in this field. The best-known example is Franco-German cooperation. But it is far from being the only one, the latest example being between Italy and Spain (Italo-Spanish Summit of 11 July 1988). Lastly, security problems are also addressed in other multilateral fora at European or Euro-Atlantic level. On the Euro-Atlantic level, there is the Eurogroup and the Independent European Programme Group (IEPG).

At the purely European level, it must be remembered that the Communities are the centre of the integration movement which is intended to lead to a European Union having, inter alia, a security dimension. In the meantime, these same Communities have competence regarding armaments cooperation in the context of their developing industrial policies. The '1992 objective' also raised the question of the future of Article 223 of the Treaty of Rome which exempts military equipment from the common market. All this explains the positions adopted by the European Parliament on defence problems and also that of Commission President Jacques Delors who recognized the rôle which WEU can play at the present stage in this field.

In the area of defence, therefore, there is something of a proliferation of cooperative arrangements and organizations; this reflects an awareness of the need to develop both a European dimension and identity in this field. But, so far, this awareness has not been given any concrete expression in the form of a single forum, in particular that of the Twelve.

In the light of the foregoing comments, the reactivated WEU may be regarded as part of the European construction process alongside the Communities and European Political Cooperation.

If the reactivated WEU is really an element in the process of building Europe, any development of substance, any significant change in the evolution of European integration, must inevitably have consequences for WEU also. For, if it were to be proved that the Twelve as a whole were now prepared, without reservation, to equip themselves with a genuine security dimension, this would be a new development which would have a strong and immediate influence on the destiny of Western European Union, which might have to ponder its future and merge into the mainstream of the European construction process. But as long as that is not the case, Western European Union remains the only forum in which its member states can reflect and confer together on their security problems. It must carry out this rôle to the full.

Likewise, WEU may also be considered as occupying a special position with respect to those cooperative projects and organizations which deal with Europe's security problems. First, because of the extremely binding alliance between its Member States provided for by the Brussels Treaty (see Article V of this Treaty). Second, because, unlike the IEPG, it has a general competence with respect to security problems. Furthermore, it has a Parliamentary Assembly with all the political weight that that confers. Finally, because its members have shown their political will to act together on security questions and to harmonize their positions.

The cost of bilateral cooperation varies – whether in terms of abandonment of sovereignty (very limited or non-existent in general), administrative expenditure and 'work cost' of the national administrations.

With regard to the Communities, and Political Cooperation in particular, its activity in the field of actual security and armaments cooperation is still too limited to be able to talk about cost.

The burgeoning of inter-European cooperative projects and organizations dealing, in varying degrees, with security problems requires their actions to be complementary and not contradictory if the participating countries are to enjoy the maximum benefit from them. This is not always a simple matter. However, the organizations concerned are making serious efforts along these lines.

The benefits in question for Belgium can be grouped under several headings:

(a) an *improvement in the defence effort efficiency* resulting, in particular, from bilateral cooperation.
(b) *a reduction in costs and an improvement* in the adaptability of its military equipment through cooperation in the production of such

equipment, and armaments in particular. Three are competent in this area:

- the IEPG;
- the European Economic Community, particularly in the framework of its industrial policies and, where appropriate, in the perspective of an organized market, if the 1992 deadline permits the obstacle raised by Article 223 of the Rome Treaty to be overcome;
- WEU. In order to reduce the risk of duplication which could be detrimental to the running of the two other organizations and the development of their activity, WEU is careful not to repeat what has been done in the other two organizations and seeks to focus on providing the political impetus – which it can and should give to their activities – its Member States being like-minded with respect to strategy and of very similar industrial background.

(c) The development of the *essential democratic debate* on security questions, at the European level, both in the European Parliament and the Parliamentary Assembly of WEU, with definite Belgian participation.

(d) *definition of specifically European strategic options* and, in terms of these, a European security identity as evidenced, for example, by the 'Platform on European Security Interests'.

(e) *increase of the Belgian influence* also within the Atlantic Alliance – and in the context of overall East-West relations.

(f) *emergence of an enhanced image of Europe* generally, also in Belgian eyes.

(g) *politically concerted and technically coordinated action* in regions which are not within the immediate security zone of Europe but which have major consequences for this security – taken in its widest meaning, viz, WEU's action in the Gulf from 20 August 1987 onwards. This action assumes all the more importance when compared with the lack of concerted European action previously in similar circumstances, viz, the 'Chaba II' affair (1978) in which the two European States mainly concerned – France and Belgium – where not only unable to produce a concerted reaction but even reacted differently, and the mining of the Red Sea (1984).

Conclusion

Belgium has always favoured a 'communitarization' of the foreign policies of the Twelve as well as the development of a security dimension among them.

It sees the following advantages for itself in such an evolution:

(a) The framework of a 'communitarized' foreign policy would give Belgium more weight in world affairs than it would have carried had it been acting in isolation on the international scene. All the positions that Belgium could have approved by the Twelve and presented by them would indeed carry the benefit of an importance they would not previously have had. The fact that, obviously, all Belgian positions would not receive the approval of the Twelve and that, as a member of the Twelve, Belgium should have to support other partners' positions, does detract from this advantage.
(b) 'Communitarized' foreign policies prevent the creation of a world Directorate by which Belgium's interests and views could be ignored. In the case of a 'communitarization' of the foreign policies of the Twelve, the West European powers that could become members of such a Directorate would have to act primarily as members of the Twelve and thus to take into account their smaller partners.
(c) In a special sector of foreign policies, common foreign trade policy positions of the Twelve have – as a whole, but with some exceptions – proved more advantageous than disadvantageous for Belgium.

The disadvantages that Belgium has met, until now, within the framework of definitions of common foreign policy decisions of the Twelve, lie essentially in the present shortcomings of the decision-making process in that field, the consequences of which being that in some cases decision-making is too slow, or because of disagreements among Member States and in the absence of means to overcome them, decisions are not taken at all.

It is Belgium's wish that the intergovernmental conferences will come up with proposals deepening the 'communitarization' of the foreign policies of the Twelve.

For Europe itself, 'communitarized' foreign policies are regarded by Belgium as a 'plus'.

(a) It is the only way, for this Europe in the process of construction, to have a decisive influence in world affairs.
(b) Furthermore, a 'europeanisation' of the Member States' policies towards Central and Eastern Europe would give these policies more balance and efficiency and would be to the benefit of both the twelve and the 'new democracies' in the East and South-East of Europe from the perspective of their progressive association or adhesion.
(c) In the state of transition we are now living in, a strengthened community of Twelve (applying also in the field of foreign policy) would be a focus of stabilization and attraction for the benefit of its member states, the transatlantic relationship and the world at large.

The development of a European security dimension is extremely difficult to achieve, caught as it is between:

- the national sovereignties (defence problems are particularly close to national sovereignties); and
- the necessary solidarity among the indispensable Atlantic Alliance.

Belgium favours, nevertheless, such an evolution. It is aware that such an evolution could, as commitments in that field become more and more compulsory, result in Belgium being called upon, through European solidarity, to take on responsibilities, roles or financial burdens that it would not necessarily have undertaken in other circumstances – which could be a disadvantage.

However:

(a) Belgium wants vigourously the emergence of a true European Union, which cannot be realized without a security dimension, and considers thus the latter as an advantage.

(b) More precisely, a foreign policy without its natural security aspect would be an incomplete, that is a lame, foreign policy. Belgium, partisan of a 'communitarization' of the foreign policies of the Twelve, cannot not consider the realization of a European security dimension – so necessary to the concretization of 'communitarized' foreign policies – as an advantage.

Note

1. The two 'Plans Fouchet' in the 1960s; the document on a European identity published in Copenhagen on 14 December 1973 by the Foreign Ministers of what were still the Nine (today the Twelve) stressing that foreign policy and security aspects have an important rôle in the achievement of a more united Europe; and the 'Tindemans Report', completed in December 1975 at the request of the member countries of the Communities (meeting as the European Council in Paris in December 1974) declaring that European Union will not be complete until it has a common defence policy. For their part both the European Parliament and the Assembly of Western European Union committed themselves long ago to work towards the establishment of such a policy – see, for instance, the draft Treaty establishing the European Union, due to the action of Mr Spinelli and approved by the European Parliament's Resolution of 14 February 1984, which is clear in its intent to include security questions within the Union's competence and particularly within the framework of those recognized with respect to international relations. Furthermore, spurred on by the European Parliament, the Commission of the European Communities, acting on the impetus given by, among others, its Vice-President, Commissioner Etienne Davignon, set about the task of bringing the production of military equipment and especially

conventional weapons within the ambit of the Communities' industrial policy. Finally, of course, the decisions of the Maastricht Summit of late 1991 clearly set up the goal of a common EC defence policy.

References

Spaak, Paul Henri (1969), *Combats inachevés*, Paris, Fayard.

Schoutheete de, Philippe (1986), *La coopération politique européenne*, 2nd edition, Bruxelles, Labor.

Chapter 10

Development policy

Youri Devuyst

The Belgian contribution to the EC's development policy: some basic figures

During recent years, Belgium spent approximately 0.45 to 0.50 per cent of its GNP on official development assistance (ODA).

The Belgian contribution to the EC's development policy has three main parts. First, Belgium finances 3.96 per cent of the 7th European Development Fund (EDF).[1] In 1991, Belgium's contribution to the EDF amounted to BF 2570 million. The EDF is the fund established in the framework of the Lomé Conventions and serves to finance projects or programmes in the Community's African, Caribbean and Pacific (ACP) partner-countries. Second, Belgium, in 1991, paid BF 35 million to the Centre for Industrial Development, which fosters the creation of joint-ventures between private companies from the Community and the developing countries. And thirdly, the Belgian Finance Ministry transfers approximately BF 2000 million to the Community on an annual basis as an obligatory contribution for development activities under the Communities budget. In addition, certain contributions to the European Investment Bank as well as to special Community programmes augment this financial effort.

According to OECD figures for 1989, Belgium's development assistance contributions to the EC accounted for approximately 16 per cent of Belgium's ODA. This represents approximately 0.08 per cent of Belgium's GNP.

Belgium tends to spend a larger percentage of ODA on EC development activities than most other small Northern member states (the Netherlands: 8.3 per cent; Denmark: 6 per cent). However, the Belgian development assistance contribution to the EC as expressed in a percentage of the country's GNP is only marginally higher than that of most other Member States (the Netherlands: also 0.08 per cent; Denmark: 0.06 per cent; FRG: 0.07 per cent; France: 0.07 per cent; U.K.: 0.06 per cent) (OECD, 1990, Table 3).

Advantages of the EC's development policy: a public policy perspective

The Belgian Government has over the years been supportive of the EC's role in the field of development policy. According to the Governmental Declaration of May 1988, which set out the government's programme at the beginning of its term, one of Belgium's priorities was 'to contribute constructively to the development of the EC's cooperation policy with developing countries'. This statement was no surprise.

As a small country, Belgium's interests in common European action in foreign policy and development cooperation are manifold.

(a) The enormous scope of the North–South problem logically leads to the conclusion that a single, small country is relatively powerless to carry out a meaningful development policy. More than any other field of action, development policy requires international cooperation, both among and between donors and recipients. According to the traditional Belgian viewpoint, the Community has a particular role to play in this domain due to the historical background of its Member States, their geographical location and economic specificity. The four Lomé Conventions form a good example of cooperation among and between donors and recipients in which the Community makes positive use of its historical, geographical and economic assets in order to create the most far-reaching and lasting series of North–South cooperation agreements ever signed (Flaesh-Mougin and Raux, 1991). None of the Community's smaller Member States could have aspired to set up a similar system on their own.

(b) For a small member state, Community action in the field of development cooperation automatically widens the scope of its involvement in North–South issues. Belgium's bilateral development policy has for a long time been little more than a Zaire, Rwanda and Burundi policy (Het Belgisch Afrika-Beleid, 1983). Zaire is a former colony, Rwanda and Burundi are former trusteeship territories. Through the Community, however, Belgium participates in a network of cooperation agreements which spans the globe.

Also, via the EC, Belgium is involved in such fundamental trade questions as the System of Generalized Preferences and the various commodity agreements. Belgium on its own would obviously be unable to keep up the same scale of involvement in North–South questions.

(c) In order to have its opinion heard in world affairs, Belgium increasingly tries to rely on the 'intermediate' Community decision-making structure. Since it has little direct power to influence decision-making on a global multilateral scale, Belgium firmly supports attempts to increase the Community's ability to speak with a single voice in international fora. Indeed, in many ways Belgium's opinions count only to the degree the Twelve manage to reach agreement on a common position.

For instance, in the International Tin Agreement, one of the commodity agreements intended to stabilize commodity prices, Belgium and Luxembourg together represent approximately 1.54 per cent of the consumer country's voting rights. However, since the Community's Member States act together within the Tin Agreement's bodies, the Community represents 27.15 per cent of the consumer country's voting rights, just ahead of the United States which possesses 26.91 per cent (O.J. L342, 3.12.1982). In fact, as a result of not casting their votes individually, the Community's Member States increase their power position and are able to participate effectively in the Agreement's decision-making.

(d) The Community also serves as a means to increase Belgium's influence in or leverage over certain developing countries.

In the first place, Belgium has used the Community to increase the pressure on a number of countries, in particular on Zaire. During the late 1980s, Belgium's relationship with President Mobutu has been severely strained. In fact, since the massacre on the campus of the University of Lubumbashi in May 1990, all cooperation between Belgium and Zaire has come to a halt. Belgium's policy, which is to foster the democratization of Zaire through the National Conference, has been effectively supported by the Twelve (see the EPC-declarations of 27 September 1991, 21 October 1991, 22 January 1992 and 17 February 1992). For instance, when Prime Minister Nguz-A Karl-I-Bond suspended the Zairean National Conference in January 1992, the Community and its Member States, on the initiative of Belgium, immediately decided to suspend their aid programmes to Zaire, except for emergency humanitarian aid, until the National Conference would fully resume and accomplish its work (EPC, 22 January 1992).

In general, the Community fully respects Belgium's special relationship with Zaire. For example, before coming forward with ideas about indicative programmes in the field of development cooperation with Zaire, the Commission always establishes an informal contact with the Belgian authorities to discuss the suitability of the proposed Community action.

In addition to receiving support regarding Zaire, Belgium has, in the second place, also benefited from the congenial environment created by the Community when it was trying to deepen and improve relations with certain countries, for instance in the Maghreb. The Community's global Mediterranean policy, the Euro-

Arab dialogue, as well as the association agreements concluded with the Maghreb countries, were seen as an important asset which facilitated the build-up of a special relationship between the Belgian Ministers of Economic Affairs and Foreign Trade and the Algerian government, which is one of Belgium's major energy suppliers (Yesilada, 1991).

(e) Finally, there often exists a positive inter-action between policy ideas developed in Belgium and by the Community. For instance, both in the Belgian Parliament (Vanvelthoven, 1990) and in the government (Geens, 1991), ideas have been advanced for the integration of human rights and good government in Belgium's development policy. Part of these ideas were inspired by the references to human rights in the Fourth Lomé Convention, signed on 15 December 1989. At the same time, the Belgian initiatives (together with similar responses in the other member states) encouraged the Commission to continue its own efforts regarding the link between human rights, democracy and development policy. As a result, the Commission drew up a policy communication on the issue, which is currently being debated by the Council and the European Parliament (Commission, 19 March 1991 and 25 March 1991; EPC, 10 December 1991).

The elements set out above explain why the Belgian government has supported, during the Intergovernmental Conference on European Political Union, the strengthening of the Community's development cooperation competences through their inclusion in the EC-pillar of the Treaty on European Union.[2]

In spite of British and Spanish objections, a new Title XVII was included in the Community Treaty. It specifies that 'Community policy in the sphere of development cooperation . . . shall be complementary to the policies pursued by the Member States'. As far as decision-making procedures are concerned, development cooperation will be dealt with in accordance with the cooperation procedure between Council and European Parliament, as provided for in Article 189c (Treaty on European Union, 7 February 1992, Title XVII).

Advantages of the EC's development policy: the perspective of the Belgian NGOs

Belgian NGOs (non-governmental organizations) have traditionally been pleading in favour of the Europeanization of development cooperation. In the first place, NGOs regard the Europeanization as a necessity in view of the enormous scope of the development problem itself. For this reason, Belgian NGOs have recently campaigned in favour of an EC policy towards the Third World debt crisis.

In the second place, Belgian NGOs seem impressed by the Community's efficient and effective administrative procedures as well as the high quality of the Commission's reflexions on development problems. The emphasis which the Community has put on collaboration with local NGOs, local education and research centres, cooperatives, unions etc. in the developing countries is also highly appreciated by the Belgian NGOs. In consequence, Belgian NGOs find the Community an interesting partner to work with. Cooperation between the Commission and the NGO is fostered through the Liaison Committee of Development NGOs to the European Communities, in which NGOs of the Twelve are represented.

In the third place, Belgian NGOs are also satisfied with the wide range of financial aid made available to them by the Community. Under normal circumstances, Belgian NGOs obtain about 10 per cent of their funds from EC sources, mainly through EC co-financing of NGO projects. For some Belgian NGOs, however, funding from the EC is much more important and reaches over 50 per cent of their entire budget. These are NGOs which have been specializing in development problems for which the Community maintains special budgets: relief for victims of apartheid, drug abuse control, AIDS prevention, environmental activities, etc.

Advantages of the EC's development policy: a Belgian business perspective

According to figures from the Belgian government of 1982 (Tindemans, 1982) and of 1990 (Bockstal, 1991), Belgian business has over the years managed to gain a significant share of the contracts financed by the EDF. Both in 1982 and 1990, the Belgian government came to the conclusion that its contribution to the EDF had a positive effect on the Belgian economy. As Table 10.1 indicates, the percentage of EDF contracts obtained by Belgian companies (excluding contracts obtained by firms from non-EC countries) exceeds the percentage of the Belgian contribution to the EDF.

The performance of Belgian business with regard to EDF contracts might be explained as follows. First, as Belgium is a small country with an open economy, its companies are used to international competition. Second, in view of the historic links between Belgium and Central Africa, some Belgian companies have achieved a particularly useful operational experience with regard to setting up programmes in ACP countries. Thirdly, the presence of the Community institutions in Brussels greatly facilitates contacts between Belgian business and the Commission. The Belgian Ministry of Foreign Trade encourages these contacts, for instance through the publication of an 'Exportmemo', a brochure which contains practical information on EDF contracts (Exportmemo, 1991).

Table 10.1 *Belgian contribution to the EDF and EDF contracts obtained by Belgian companies, 30 September 1990*

	Belgian contribution to the EDF, in per cent (a)	EDF contracts obtained by Belgian companies, in per cent (b)
EDF 4	6.25	8.1
EDF 5	5.9	6.6
EDF 6	3.95	9.7
EDF 7	3.96	(c)

Source: adapted from Bockstal, 1991
(a) The Belgian share among the EC-12
(b) The Belgian share among the EC-12, excluding contracts obtained by non-EC states
(c) Not yet in operation.

Disadvantages of the EC's development policy

This is neither the place to criticize the EC's development policy in general, nor to elaborate on the negative consequences for the developing countries of certain elements of the Community's trade or agricultural policy (for a critical annual review of the EC's development policy, see Stevens et al., 1981 and subsequent years). It must be said, however, that during the ratification debate on Lomé IV in the Belgian parliament, it was pointed out that the Lomé agreements had resulted neither in a significant improvement of economic and social welfare in the ACP countries nor in an expansion of EC imports from the ACP countries. On the contrary, in 1975 when Lomé I went into effect, EC imports from ACP countries amounted to 8 per cent of total Community imports. In 1987, that figure had fallen to 3.8 per cent (Sénat de Belgique, 7 May 1991).

From a purely Belgian perspective, the first major problem with EC development cooperation is of a budgetary nature. Seen in absolute figures, Belgium's contribution to the EDF has gone up from BF 1752.4 million in 1985 to BF 2570.8 million in 1991. In 1992, Belgium's contribution to the EDF is expected to increase again, to BF 2843.7 million. According to the so-called Delors II package, the Community's financial effort in the external sphere should be doubled between 1992 (ECU 3.6 billion) and 1997 (Delors asks for ECU 6.3 billion) (Commission, 19 February 1992).

The sharp increase in the Community's financial demands on the member states is understandable in view of the many external challenges which Western Europe is currently facing. Against the background of an annual budget deficit of 6.3 per cent of GNP and a total debt figure of 129.4 per cent of GNP, Belgium, however, will have a hard time meeting the Community's demands for additional financial means. Indeed, Community demands come at a time when Belgium will have to cut public expenditure severely in view of the criteria established in the framework of the European Economic and Monetary Union.

The second problem with regard to the EC's development cooperation concerns Belgium's impact on the Community's policy-making. Belgium's General Administration for Development Cooperation seems insufficiently organized to monitor the Community's development policy in detail. As a result, it is incapable of evaluating its financial input in the Community's development action to the extent it would prefer. Consequently, genuine fears exist within the Belgian General Administration for Development Cooperation that Belgium's development cooperation funds might flow increasingly to a Community policy over which the Belgian Administration has little or no say.

In the same context, Belgium is extremely unhappy about the decision, taken on the initiative of Germany, not to discuss so-called 'small' EDF-projects (with a value of less than ECU 2 million) in the EDF-Committee any longer. These 'small' EDF-projects are simply notified to the Committee after their adoption by the Commission. For a small country like Belgium, ECU 2 million is a considerable amount.

Moreover, through the discussion in the EDF-Committee, interesting information became available to the Belgian representative both regarding the value of the project and the developments in the ACP-country concerned.

While Belgium is often bound to 'follow' decisions taken on the initiative of the large countries within the Community, it seems very difficult for a small country to see its own ideas transformed into decisions. For instance, Belgium's proposal to develop a European public export-credit insurance office, which would broaden the financial basis of export-credit insurance operations (this is especially important for the smaller countries), was rejected by the Community's large member states.

Overall balance

In the field of development cooperation, the advantage of EC membership outweigh the disadvantages for Belgium. Via the Community, Belgium is able to participate in a network of cooperation agreements which spans the globe, thereby widening the scope of its involvement in North–South issues. Belgium on its own could never have aspired to set up a similar system. Moreover, in order to have its opinions heard in world affairs, Belgium depends in large measure on a Community speaking with one voice.

In addition to these considerations, the Community has provided Belgium with concrete support, for instance in its conflict with Zaire. Also, Belgian NGOs active in the field of development cooperation as well as Belgian business benefit without question from the Community's development policy.

Against the background of Belgium's general support for a Common Foreign and Security Policy and because of the enormous scale of the development problem, the gradual transfer of development cooperation to the European level should not be resisted by Belgian officials. The Belgian development administration should consequently be restructured so as to prepare itself adequately for the Europeanization of development cooperation. Instead of looking backward, Belgium's administration should be inspired by the example of the Belgian development NGOs which seem successful in their gradual reorientation towards the European level. For only by preparing the Europeanization adequately will Belgium (possibly in a Benelux framework) secure a significant place for itself in the EC's decision-making structure.

Notes

1. In order to put Belgium's 3.96 per cent in perspective, it is interesting to know that the share of the other member states in the 7th EDF is distributed as follows: Denmark: 2.07; France: 24.36; Germany: 25.96; Greece: 1.22; Ireland: 0.54; Italy: 12.96; Luxembourg: 0.19; Netherlands: 5.56; Portugal: 0.87; Spain: 5.89; United Kingdom: 16.37.
2. It must be noted that development cooperation, as such, had no specific basis in the EEC Treaty. Community activities in the field of development cooperation have been based on EEC Articles of a general or commercial policy nature.

References

Aktiviteitenverslag 1990 (1991), Brussels: Algemeen Bestuur Ontwikkelingssamenwerking.

Bockstal, Elie (1991), *Rapport fait au nom de la Commission des Relations Extérieures*, Sénat de Belgique, Session de 1990–1991, No. 1299–2, 17 April.

Commission of the European Communities (19 March 1991), *Human Rights, Democracy and Development*, Brussels: Information Memo.

Commission of the European Communities (25 March 1991), *Human Rights, Democracy and Development Cooperation Policy*, Brussels: SEC(91)61 def.

Commission of the European Communities (19 February 1992), 'From the Single Act to Maastricht and Beyond. The Means to Match our Ambitions', *Agence Europe*, No. 1762/63.

EPC (27 September 1991), *Declaration on Zaire*, Brussels: Press Release P. 92/91.

EPC (21 October 1991), *Declaration on Zaire*, Brussels: Press Release P. 102/91.

EPC (10 December 1991), *Press Statement on the Activity of the Community and its Member States in the Field of Human Rights in 1991*, Brussels: Press Release P. 127/91.

EPC (22 January 1992), *Declaration on Zaire*, Brussels: Press Release P. 11/92.

EPC (17 February 1992), *Declaration on Zaire*, Brussels: Press Release P. 21/92.

Exportmemo (1991), Brussels: Ministerie van Buitenlandse Zaken, Buitenlandse Handel en Ontwikkelingssamenwerking.

Flaesch-Mougin, Catherine and Jean Raux (1991), 'From Lomé III to Lomé IV: EC-ACP Relations', in Leon Hurwitz and Christian Lequesne (eds), *The State of the European Community*, Longman: Lynne Rienner, pp. 343–357.

Geens, André (1991), *Reflectienota over Ontwikkelingssamenwerking en Mensenrechten*, Brussels: Kabinet van de Minister van Ontwikkelingssamenwerking

Het Belgisch Afrika-Beleid (1983), Brussels: Ministerie van Buitenlandse Zaken, Buitenlandse Handel en Ontwikkelingssamenwerking.

OECD (1990), *Examen de l'aide de la Belgique par le CAD*, Paris: OECD SG/Press (90)52, 18 September.

O.J. (Official Journal of the European Communities), L 342, 3.12.1982, p. 30.

Sénat de Belgique (7 May 1991), *Annales parlementaires*, pp. 2064–2068.

Stevens, Christopher et al. (1981 and subsequent years), *EEC and the Third World: A Survey*, London: Hodder Stoughton.

Tindemans, Leo (1982), 'Het nieuwe perspectief: de Belgische politiek inzake buitenlandse economische betrekkingen', *Krachtlijnen van de Buitenlandse Politiek van België*, Brussels: Ministerie van Buitenlandse Zaken, Buitenlandse Handel en Ontwikkelingssamenwerking.

'Treaty on European Union' (7 February 1992), *Agence Europe*, No. 1759/60.

Vanvelthoven, Louis (1990), *Proposition de loi relative à l'évaluation de la politique de cooperation au développement en fonction du respect des droits de l'homme*, Chambre des Représentants de Belgique, Session ordinaire 1989–1990, No. 1201/1, 21 May.

Yesilada, Birlon Ali (1991), 'The EC's Mediterranean Policy' in Leon Hurwitz and Christian Lequesne (eds), *The State of the European Community*, Longman: Lynne Rienner, pp. 359–372.

PART III: THE POLITICAL AND LEGAL SYSTEM

Chapter 11

Sovereignty and supranationality

Philippe de Schoutheete

Historical background

In the long term the foreign policy of each state is largely determined by geography and history, the interplay of economic forces and political influence, which constitutes the fundamental and lasting interests of nations. But in the short and medium term they are shaped and formulated by individual statesmen, some of whom by their stature and their power of conviction have an influence which lasts beyond their term of office and even their lifetime. Such is the case of the European policy of Belgium which, in the second half of the century, has been heavily influenced by the position initially taken by a generation of postwar political figures with prewar political experience, foremost amongst whom was Paul-Henri Spaak. 'Il n'est aucune des grandes entreprises de l'après-guerre auxquelles notre pays a été associé, dans laquelle il (P.H. Spaak) n'ait participé de manière souvent décisive. Il avait compris et senti que la place de la Belgique était dans un contexte plus large que le cadre national. Elle ne pouvait se développer que si elle devenait européenne' (Simonet 1986: 136).

Such had not always been Spaak's views. In 1936 Belgium, which, since the First World War, had had close relationships with France and Britain, decided to observe a strict neutrality. Spaak, then Foreign Minister, told Parliament in July that he wanted one thing only: a foreign policy wholly and entirely Belgian ('une politique étrangère exclusivement et intégralement belge') and this sentence was repeated by Prime Minister Van Zeeland in September and King Leopold III in October. Spaak was the prime mover behind this policy of 'free hands' as he admits in his memoirs: 'On estime généralement que je suis le Ministre responsable de la politique d'indépendance pratiquée par la Belgique en matiére internationale de 1936 à 1940' (Spaak 1969: 40). This policy was to prove a dismal failure. It provoked sour criticism from the Western allies without protecting the country, when the time came, from a fully fledged German 'blitzkrieg'.

The military weaknesses of the Western democracies were such that even if Belgium had accepted the responsibilities of a military alliance the results would probably not have been very different in the summer of 1940. But recrimination is a by-product of defeat, and, when defeat was at hand, recrimination and abuses were heaped on Belgium, not least by the French Prime Minister. A policy which leads to military occupation by your enemies and abuse by your allies cannot be called a success. For the second time in a generation Belgium was submitted to foreign rule, a victim of rivalries between its neighbours, as a result of a chain of events over which it had been unable to exert any effective influence. The morale of the country was deeply bruised and its very existence seemed in danger. Clearly some conclusions had to be drawn.

If the political picture was disastrous, the economic angle was less than satisfactory. As an early player in the industrial revolution, Belgium had known a relatively high level of prosperity in the nineteenth century and in the immediate aftermath of the First World War. Capitalizing on its geographical location, its colonial empire, its relatively low wages and hard-working population, the country had built an export-oriented economy which prospered in the free-trade and stable monetary world of the 'Belle époque'. The economic crisis of the 1930s put an end to that. In a world of exchange controls, competitive devaluations, high tariffs, protectionism (tending to autarchy in the case of communist and fascist regimes) an export-oriented economy is bound to encounter more difficulties even than others. Efforts undertaken in the late 1930s, with the help of the Dutch and Scandinavians, to re-establish some measure of openness and reason in European trade, had not been notably successful. Here too some conclusions had to be drawn.

In the depressing inactivity of exile, or in the enforced inactivity of occupied territory, the political, administrative and economic establishment of Belgium had time to reflect on these events and came not surprisingly to a common body of views which were to shape postwar policy. These views were not elaborated in detail, nor was there full and formal agreement on them, but in the main outlines they can be summarized as follows (Gotovitch 1987: 39–50):

- good relationships between Belgium's neighbours are not only desirable: they are essential to the survival of the country;
- it is impossible for a country the size of Belgium, in its geographical location and in the circumstances of the twentieth century, to safeguard its independence in isolation;
- it is extremely difficult, if not impossible, in these circumstances for such a country to attain economic prosperity in isolation;
- in other words, changing technology (even the technologies of the 1930s) and increasing interdependence severely limit the capacity of the country to exert effective influence on its own destiny.

The inescapable conclusion was that sovereignty and absolute independence were illusory concepts and that postwar policy needed to be based on far-reaching international cooperation and regional economic integration. As early as 1942 a document submitted to the Belgian government in exile in London talked about 'l'organisation de la Communauté Européenne dans l'ordre et la liberté' (Spaak 1969: 156). In the winter of 1944 Spaak submitted to the British Foreign Office a note on the military, political and economic cooperation in postwar Europe and had an unsuccessful conversation with Churchill on the subject. 'Il n'était pas séduit par l'idée d'organiser l'Europe occidentale. Mes projets d'économies intégrées lui semblaient, je crois, chimériques' (Spaak 1969: 164). This was not to be the last time that Belgian and British Ministers would disagree on the level and urgency of European integration. But other parties were more receptive: in 1943 the governments in exile signed the first Benelux agreement and in April 1945, before the end of the war, the economic union of the three Benelux countries was signed in the Hague. Baron (later Count) Jean-Charles Snoy et d'Oppuers, former Secretary General of the Ministry of Economic Affairs, had presided, during the war, in occupied Belgium, a clandestine reflection group on economic policy. He had had contacts with similar groups in The Netherlands and France and had come to much the same conclusions on the necessity of international economic cooperation (Snoy 1989: 47). He was to be, together with Spaak, the major Belgian negotiator of the Treaty of Rome which he also signed.

In the immediate postwar period, the first attempts at economic cooperation, in the traditional form of intergovernmental negotiations, showed how difficult it was to move forward. Nationalism and the pursuit of shortsighted self-interest created an atmosphere of failure and mutual suspicion reminiscent of the late 1930s. However, the discreet and persuasive efforts of Jean Monnet were gradually winning over the French and German governments to commit themselves to a totally different idea: a federal approach to the problem of Europe. After his speech of 9 May 1950 suggesting the Coal and Steel Community, Schuman was asked to comment on his proposal: his answer was: 'C'est un saut dans l'inconnu' (Monnet 1976: 441).

Belgium's position

'It is the fate of small and relatively weak countries to be trampled on when their large neighbours make war and to have their interests squeezed when these neighbours make up . . . The beauty of the Schuman and subsequent proposals was that they held out the prospect of guarantees of equality undreamt of in previous attempts at European Cooperation' (Tugendhat 1986: 36). This perceptive comment by the former British Commissioner, Christopher Tugendhat, admirably expresses the obvious merits, from a Belgian point of view, of the novel suggestions put forward in 1950 by the French Foreign Minister. They seemed to offer lasting guarantees of Franco-German reconciliation and economic development in a framework open to smaller states and where they would be listened to. In exchange, concessions had to be made in the field of economic sovereignty to a new 'High Authority'. But economic sovereignty seemed an empty concept, so the answer was clear.

Less than a month after the Schuman proposal, Spaak wrote a leading article on it in *Le Soir*: 'Le 9 mai 1950 sera peut-être une date d'une importance capitale dans l'histoire de l'organisation européenne et de la construction de la paix . . . Voyons seulement la grandeur de l'idée et cherchons de bonne foi à la réaliser . . . Que M. Schuman le sache, l'opinion publique est avec lui, elle reste sensible aux idées généreuses et elle est plus prête qu'on ne le croit à les soutenir courageusement même au prix de certains sacrifices' (La pensée . . . 1980: 223–6).

In the 40 years which have elapsed since the Schuman proposals, Belgian authorities have systematically supported the line initially taken by Spaak. Successive governments of different political hues have committed themselves strongly to European integration and accepted its ambitious long-term goals. At turning points in the history of the European community, Belgian statesmen or high officials have played key roles precisely because their commitment to the common (as opposed to the national) interest was not in doubt: Spaak and Snoy at the Messina conference and the subsequent negotiations; Spaak again in the 'empty chair' crisis of 1965; Davignon at the birth of political cooperation in 1970; Tindemans on European Union in 1975. Innumerable ministerial speeches and governmental declarations could be quoted to this effect.

This attitude was not entirely unopposed. Strong opposition against the Coal and Steel Community was voiced initially by the Belgian coal and steel industry, and, for very different reasons by the Belgian Communist party (Dumoulin 1987: 23). Spaak, who had kept his colleagues in government largely uninformed of the negotiations leading to the Rome treaty, had serious last-minute difficulties in convincing Prime Minister Van Acker. He explains in his memoirs that after long discussions and threats of resignation Van Acker gave in 'more out of friendship for myself than from real conviction (Spaak 1969: 97). Doubts were expressed in Parliament, both from the left and the right, as to the compatibility of the European treaties with the text of the Belgian constitution; and King Baudouin himself had to be convinced on this score (Snoy 1989: 119).

The beneficial effects of the first steps in European integration, the power of conviction of its advocates and the passage of time overcame these initial oppositions. There is no doubt that, with very few exceptions, a constant political line can be seen over the years, irrespective of the political parties in power. This line can be summarized as follows:

1 Belgium adopts European integration as an aim in itself. She supports new imaginative proposals when they are put forward in the Community framework: the Werner and Tindemans reports, the European monetary system, the Single European Act, the Delors report on EMU, etc. She sets high and ambitious goals for Europe and sees them in a political perspective. Baron van der Meulen, who for more than 20 years was Permanent Representative of Belgium to the EC, expressed this as follows: 'European integration for us also meant a political engagement which, via growing unification, should finally emerge into a European Union dealing with all problems that could be more easily solved in a community than on national level. This clearly implied that priority was to be given to the community beyond national political perspectives' (Verbeke 1981: 16).
2 Belgium supports the supranational elements in the European power structure. She favours delegation of power to the Commission and therefore sides with that institution in the repetitive debates on 'comitology'. She has also repeatedly favoured increased power for the European Parliament. In Council, Belgium is one of the few Member States who has never accepted, used or threatened to use the interpretation of the so-called 'Luxemburg compromise' of 1965 which, in the opinion of some governments, entitles them to block majority voting on issues of vital national interest. Van der Meulen puts it as follows: 'Belgium has always been a convinced advocate of the "Supranational Europe", in other words a Europe organized in such a way that final decision can be taken only by a majority vote, without veto power' (Verbeke 1981: 27).
3 Belgium mistrusts proposals going in the direction of mere intergovernmental cooperation, such as the Fouchet plan in the early 1960s. She tends to see in them a reactionary reversal to the traditions of prewar diplomacy, a dangerous weakening of the Community framework and the threat of a 'directoire' of the bigger European partners. When intergovernmental cooperation seems to be the only way forward, Belgium then tries to keep the Community as closely involved as possible. This has been her constant attitude in political cooperation, until the London report of 1981 finally admitted the Commission as a full partner in all activities of EPC. This has also been the rationale behind the insistance, strongly formulated by Simonet in 1976, that the Community as such should be present at Western economic summit meetings. Belgium also insisted that the Commission should be closely associated with the Eureka initiatives (on technology and, more recently, audio-visual activities) both of whose secretariats have for that reason been situated in Brussels.

This continuity in European aspirations was expressed by Leo Tindemans in 1987, when speaking in Rome as President-in-office on the occasion of the thirtieth anniversary of the European Treaties. Looking back on the first formative years he says: 'The only cause for regret now is that more was not done in those heroic days, that they did not go further along the road to integration' (*Guidelines* 1989: 24).

Supranationality and national identity

In the preface to a booklet on Belgium and the European Community, Henri Simonet, then Minister for Foreign Affairs, mentions various explanations for the strong European commitment of successive Belgian governments. He writes: 'Peut-être aussi nos difficultés internes, la fragilité ressentie de certaines structures nationales, ont-elles contribué chez nous à accroître l'enthousiasme pour l'aventure européenne' (La Belgique 1979: 5). This explanation seems to have been shared by de Gaulle who writes in his memoirs: 'Comment la Belgique, tendue à maintenir en un tout la juxtaposition des Flamands et des Wallons, depuis que, par compromis, les puissances rivales parvinrent à faire d'elle un Etat, pourrait-elle se consacrer sincèrement à autre chose?' (de Gaulle 1970: 192).

Various historical explanations have been given for the specific nature of the Belgian state (see also chapter 18). For some, like de Gaulle, it is the artificial creation of nineteenth-century power politics. For others, like Henri Pirenne, it is the modern form of a deep, ancient solidarity going back to the Middle Ages. Whatever explanation we prefer, the fact is that Belgium, a bilingual state at the crossroads of Europe, long used by its neighbours as a preferred battlefield, has always had a lesser degree of national self-consciousness and identity than other more monolithic and less-exposed nations. 'L'identité nationale de la Belgique est moins affirmée que celle de beaucoup d'autres et singulièrement de ses voisins les plus immédiats', writes Henri Simonet (1986: 138).

This explains why there has been little trace in Belgium of the conflict between national identity and the supranational concept which has been, over the years, so characteristic of the European debate in France (from Michel Debré to Pierre Chevènement) or in Britain (from Tony Benn to Margaret Thatcher). When de Gaulle talks disparagingly of the 'soi-disant exécutifs, installés à la tête des organismes communs en vertu des illusions d'intégration qui sévissaient avant mon retour' (1970: 192) he may strike a nationalistic chord in French public opinion. In Belgium the argument carries little weight when compared to the security and economic prosperity that the integration process provides.

Since the late 1950s and 1960s growing nationalist movements, first in Flanders, then in Wallonia, have contributed to a further weakening of the feeling of Belgian national identity. Successive devolutions of power to the component parts of the Belgian state have developed, at the same time as, in other fields, power was being devolved from Member States to the European Community. These movements are not seen, or felt, to be contradictory or mutually exclusive. Rather it can be said that the European Economic Community, and its gradual integration process, provides a safety-net whereby greater regional autonomy can be pursued without the risk of disastrous economic consequences. Practical difficulties can and do arise, but a major economic breakdown is excluded by the existence of the Community structure.

This may explain the surprising fact that even the more radical and nationalistic Flemish or Walloon political movements have not questioned the European integration process. In fact José Happart, who has come to embody the more radical Walloon aspirations, is himself a member of the European Parliament and founder of a movement called 'Wallonie, région d'Europe'. In Belgium the supranational concept does not seem to clash with the feelings of national or regional identity. In fact a feeling of European identity complements national or regional attachment for a significant number of Belgians. Fernand Herman, another Belgian member of the European Parliament, writes: 'l'Europe est devenue mon pays et la Belgique ma province. Ce sont des allégeances ou des fidélités parfaitement compatibles' (Herman 1989: 174).

National identity and community of values

A sustained effort of convergence and unification, over more than a generation, by countries divided by language, levels of prosperity and climate, whose history has been more conflictual than consensual, is a remarkable phenomenon. This could not have been possible without a pre-existing community of values, common views on the basic elements of human society. The birth, growth and extension of the European Community was made possible because the Member States shared convictions and practices in matters of democratic government, human rights and the rule of law. These were implicit from the beginning, long before the European Council at Copenhagen in 1978 saw fit to enshrine them in a declaration on democracy. The successive accessions of Greece, Spain and Portugal were understood by all parties as confirmation and consolidation of their newly acquired democratic character. Something similar explains the magnetic appeal of the Community in Eastern Europe in recent months.

Outside the political and legal concepts, there is also a common cultural heritage, built over the centuries from Athens, Rome and Florence, to Oxford and Paris, Salamanca, Bruges and Heidelberg. But European culture and democratic government also exist outside the Community in Vienna and Stockholm for example. They are the common cement of the Council of Europe. So what is specific to the European Community?

In the views of Belgian political leaders, the specificity of the European Community has been the common will to defend shared values by an organized collective effort, in an institutional framework implying concessions on national sovereignty: 'To lay the foundation for institutions which will give direction to a destiny hence forward shared' says the preamble to the Paris Treaty in 1951. This is what Spaak, when signing the Rome Treaty, called: 'la plus grande transformation volontaire et dirigée de l'histoire de l'Europe' (1969: 99). This is what the Davignon report, at the birth of political cooperation in 1970, calls 'to give shape to the will for political union which has not ceased to further the progress of the European Communities'. Tindemans, in the introductory letter to his report on European Union, writes in 1975: 'It is in fact by means of institutions which have been strengthened and improved that the Union will be able to give increasing expression to its own dynamism.'

Mrs Thatcher, in her Bruges speech in 1988, was right to recall that countries outside the Community are also European. But who has built, in the course of the years, the world's major trading power, capable of addressing the United States or Japan as an entity? Who has built, in the course of the years, a centre of political cohesion and vision which now serves as the major factor of stability in the whole continent, an anchor in troubled waters? The answer is: successive governments of Community countries, including, albeit reluctantly at times, the British government, acting through their common institutions and giving to those institutions the necessary powers, at the cost of some national sovereignty. This, countries outside the Community have not wanted to do.

Certainly the feeling that an important transformation has been achieved, that an ongoing process is gradually leading the Community to a political system, as yet indeterminate but at times already operational, going beyond the nation-state concept as it evolved in the last two centuries, is prevalent in the political discussions in Belgium. It serves as a long-term goal for a fragile country.

In sum, it can be said that the European Community has brought to Belgium:

- a durable solution to the Franco–German rivalry which twice threatened the very existence of the country;
- a means of greater participation in economic and political decisions, formerly settled by direct contact between major European powers;
- a long-term goal which makes it easier to surmount internal contradictions and the inadequacies of the nation-state concept as applied to Belgium (see chapter 4).

Though not articulately voiced nor perhaps consciously perceived by the majority, these considerations undoubtedly play an important role in the European commitment of a vast majority of Belgians.

References

Dumoulin, M. (1987) *La Belgique et les débuts de la construction européenne*, Brussels, CIACO.

Gaulle de, Charles (1970), *Mémoires d'espoir*, Paris, Plon.

Gotovitch, José (1987) 'Perspectives européennes dans la résistance et à Londres durant la guerre', in *La Belgique et les débuts de la construction européenne*, Brussels, CIACO.

Guidelines of Belgium external policy, Texts and documents (1989), Ministry of Foreign Affairs, no. 197.

Herman, Fernand (1989) *Europe mon pays*, Brussels.

La Belgique et la Communauté européenne, Texts and documents (1979), Ministry of Foreign Affairs, no. 317.

La pensée européenne et atlantique de P.H. Spaak (1980), Brussels, Goemaere.

Monnet, Jean (1976), *Mémoires*, Paris, Fayard.

Simonet, Henri (1986) *Je n'efface rien et je recommence*, Brussels, Didier Hatier.

Snoy et d'Oppuers, Jean-Charles (1989) *Rebatir l'Europe*, Gembloux, Duculot.

Spaak, Paul-Henri (1969) *Combats inachevés*, Paris, Fayard.

Tugendhat, Christopher (1986) *Making sense of Europe*, London, Viking.

Verbeke, G. (1981) (ed.) *Belgium and Europe*, proceedings of the International Franqui-colloquium (Brussels, Ghent 12–14 November 1980), Brussels.

Chapter 12

Democracy and the rule of law

J.P. De Bandt

In analysing the impact of Belgium's membership in the European Community countries on its political and legal system, attention should first be given to some of the underlying facts of the Belgium polity. The Belgian constitution of 1830 – the oldest written constitution of the twelve member countries of the EC – created a liberal (bourgeois) system of government, highly centralized, almost Jacobin in its concept, inspired by French thinking. It contained a bill of rights which at the time many scholars heralded as a model of progress.

The Belgian constitution and thus the institutional framework of Belgian democracy did not undergo any noteworthy change until 1970, when the classical model of the centralized state ended and a process of devolution of powers from the centralized state to newly created regions began. This process of devolution, which started with the constitutional reform of 1970, was followed by two major reforms in 1980 and 1988, and a third phase of the last 1988 reform is currently in preparation.

With this background in mind, this chapter will examine the impact of the European Community on democracy and the rule of law, Chapter 13 will deal with the primacy of Community law and Chapter 14 will consider the impact on state organizations.

The concept of costs and benefits is easier to measure and to quantify in fields such as economics, intra-Community trade in goods and services, investments and the free circulation of persons than it is with respect to government and legal systems, where qualitative judgements must replace statistics, figures and graphs.

Democracy

The influence of the European Community on democracy in Belgium is difficult to measure. The principle of democracy is not, as such, described in the Belgian constitution and except for the basic architecture in the 1830 Constitution, such as the separation of the three powers, the bill of rights, the 'trias politica', the parliamentary form of government and the plurality voting introduced by the constitutional amendment of 1919, the content of today's democracy in Belgium has been built over the years through a series of legislative enactments. These include the social welfare state in 1946; the protection of citizens against illegal conduct of public authority through the creation of the Council of State in 1948 (the highest administrative court in Belgium); the protection of the consumer; the protection of the environment; the protection of the poor (minimex) and the new principle of equal treatment contained in the new 1988 constitutional reform.

We cannot infer, however, that the European Community has had any decisive influence on democracy and the Belgian framework of democratic institutions. There is instead a particular characteristic of Belgium's democracy which is relevant here and should be emphasized. Belgian political culture is not strongly participative. Individuals who wish to participate may do so through membership of a political party or a pressure group. Belgian polity has evolved since the end of the Second World War towards a consociational or consensus model in which political parties – which have no constitutional or legal existence – and representative organizations of labour and employers play a predominant role in the decision-making process. Belgium is, in this respect, the only country of the European Community (except perhaps for The Netherlands, but to a much lesser degree) where this consociational model has achieved such a degree of sophistication.

Therefore it is worth observing that the European Community as an institutional model has many features in common with the Belgian consociational model; the composition of the Commission is an example where all European political families are represented. The same holds true, but for different reasons, in the Council of Ministers. The organization and the function of the Economic and Social Council and the role of labour and employers' organizations in this Council show striking similarities to the Belgian model.

However, this is not to suggest that there was a direct influence or impact of the Belgian postwar institutional model on the European Community. There is certainly no evidence which points in that direction. This is probably due to the fact that Europe, like Belgium, is a conglomerate of great diversity and that diversity – as in Belgium – inevitably leads to consensus building. It would also be erroneous to conclude that the Belgian model has had any influence on the setting and organization of the European institutions.

Returning to the impact of the European Community on Belgian principles of democracy – and leaving aside the impact with respect to the rule of law, which will be reviewed later in this chapter – we could conclude that this influence has not been substantial. As will be briefly analysed, in one area – on the cost side – the transfer of powers and competences to the European Community has raised serious questions with respect to the democratic legitimacy of decisions. Decisions which, before their transfer, were taken by a democratically elected Parliament are now taken at Community level by a Council of Ministers which unfortunately thus far lacks democratic legitimacy. Intergovernmental conferences in various fields of law without any parliamentary control take too many decisions.

On the 'benefit' side, two areas can be earmarked where the European Community has clearly paved the way for new rules and concepts in the Belgian legal order: the principle of equality between men and women and the protection of the environment. Also on the 'benefit side', another major influence is that of the European Convention on Human Rights signed in Rome and approved by the Belgian law of 13 March 1955.

The influence of the European Court on Human Rights on Belgian legislative and judicial power is considerable. This 'European' bill of rights, however, falls outside the scope of this analysis as it is not strictly a European Community institution. Nevertheless, it cannot be ignored because of its far-reaching process in Belgium in the protection of rights and on due process rules. The European bill of rights undoubtedly had more influence on the Belgian legal order than the Joint Declaration on Fundamental Rights adopted by the European Parliament, the Council and the Commission on 8 April 1977.[1] The European Council, in its Declaration on Democracy of 7—8 April 1978, confirmed its respect for fundamental rights and freedom.[2] These declarations have generally been seen as reactions to the ruling of the German Federal Constitutional Court of 1970.[3] The Joint Declaration is to be seen as a uniform Community-wide definition of fundamental rights; it constitutes a system distinct from the national constitutional principles on the protection of individuals within the scope and objectives of Community interests. They have thus far not been perceived by Belgian courts as a new set of fundamental rights, which require direct application in the Belgian legal order.

The European Court on Human Rights has played a major role in the Belgian judiciary which traditionally showed a certain reluctance to enforce elementary due-process rules. Elementary rules relating to the public character of hearings, especially in disciplinary matters, or the right of defence, have been insisted upon through landmark decisions of the European Court on Human Rights. A separate and detailed study — which falls outside the scope of this study — should be undertaken to describe the decisive influence of the Strasbourg Court on Belgian behaviour and attitudes in the field of democracy.

The 'cost': the democratic legitimacy of the European institutions

In Belgian constitutional law, any state authority acquires its legitimacy from the nation (the citizens). Article 25: 'All powers emanate from the

Nation'. Doubts arose in the 1950s about the constitutionality of treaties, which would transfer competences to international organizations. The Council of State (which renders opinions on any bill to be approved by Parliament) had formulated objections with respect to the transfer of sovereignty to international organizations.[4] Article 25 was then modified by the addition of an article 25bis which today reads as follows: 'The exercise of given competences can be attributed by a treaty or a law to institutions of public international law.'

The European Communities are institutions of public international law within the meaning of Article 25bis because of their formal creation by treaty. In fact, no judicial effect has been given to this new constitutional provision since the primacy of Community Law, as will be seen later, was established by the Belgian Supreme Court without any references to Belgian constitutional law. Article 25bis, however, is important in the sense that it constitutes the only constitutional amendment caused by membership in the EC. This constitutional amendment gives full legitimacy to the transfer of sovereignty and the devolution of powers to the European Community. In turn, serious criticism has been voiced not about the transfer of sovereignty, but about the transfer of sovereignty to institutions that lack any democratic legitimacy.

In the European Community, the legislative powers are vested in the Council and the Commission. Neither of these has a direct democratic legitimacy of its own, and neither constitutes a specific legislative body or authority. In Belgium, both legislative chambers, the Chamber of Representatives and the Senate, have a clear democratic mandate.

The absence of democratic legitimacy is obviously one of the major democratic 'costs' of the present European institutional framework and is increasingly resented by the Belgian electorate. Belgian political parties are therefore advocating almost unanimously that the European Parliament, whose legitimacy is based on general elections, be given more substantial legislative powers.

Parliamentary control of government is another feature of the Belgian democratic system. Governmental functions within the EC are exercised by both the Commission and the Council. No similar control is exercised by the European Parliament on the Council and Commission. The European Parliament has a number of instruments for the exercise of such control such as the right to put written or oral questions to the Commission,[5] the right to discuss the general report of the Commission[6] and the no-confidence vote.[7]

Yet the one major competence that the European Parliament lacks in comparison to the Belgian system is the right to control the appointment of the members of the executive. The same remark applies to other member countries, where the legislative institutions are based on democratic legitimacy.

The 'benefits' in terms of democracy

Environmental law

It is fair to say that environmental law is fundamentally rooted in the right of human beings to require that nature and the environment – in its broadest sense – be protected. In this sense, environmental law has become a fundamental part of the bill of rights of any democratic state. There are few domains where the influence of the European Community has been felt so strongly as in environmental matters.

It would be beyond the scope of this analysis to trace back the history of the EC environmental policy and describe the continuous flow of EC legislation over the years. Most of the Belgian legislation in this field is, in fact, inspired or mandated by EC directives. Referring to 'Belgian' legislature is misleading in the sense that almost all competences relating to the environment have been transferred to the three Belgian regions. The competence in environmental matters was transferred in the constitutional reform of 1980 to the Flemish region and to the Walloon region; the 1988 constitutional reform transferred the same competences to the Brussels region (see Chapter 5).

This devolution process to the regions has caused considerable delays in the implementation of EC directives. The Commission announced in its yearly review for 1989 of the EC environmental policy that out of the 368 violations of directives by Member States (there are a total of 60 directives), Belgium and Italy scored the maximum. There are 46 procedures against Belgium for alleged violations of EC environmental rules, especially in the field of waste and water pollution. Belgium's poor performance is primarily attributed to the federalization process and the complicated system of conflict resolution between the regions. This is not to say that the influence of European integration has not been decisive in Belgian environmental policies. The influence has been substantial and is still growing steadily.

Equality between men and women

On another basic principle in a democratic state, equality between men and women, the EC Commission has greatly influenced both the legislature and the courts in Belgium (see also Chapter 16). The EEC Treaty contains two sets of rules relating to labour law:

- Articles 48–51 relating to the free circulation of workers and, in particular, Article 51 authorizing the council to establish rules for migrant workers;
- Articles 117–128 relating to the social policy of the Community and more specifically Article 119 which establishes the principle of equal salary for men and women.

A number of important directives, which began in 1975, have laid down the rules of equality between men and women. It started with equal remuneration, to include, at a later stage, equal access to employment, training work conditions, social security, unemployment, transfer of business and maternity leave – a huge programme which has been backed by extensive case law in the European Court of Justice.

These basic principles were introduced in Belgium by law on 4 August 1978, which in turn gave rise to extensive case law in Belgian courts. Because of the primacy and direct applicability of Community law in Belgium, courts can also rely directly on the Treaty and in particular Article 119 thereof, to give full force and effect to the rule of equality. The influence of the EC on Belgian law and practice is evident here. A basic democratic principle has been introduced in the Belgian legal system through European Community principles.[8]

The rule of law

The 'rule of law' is a broad concept which refers to the 'rechtstaatsprinzip'. Some Member States of the European Community have expressed reference to this principle in their constitutions. The Belgian Constitution does not contain any provision which guarantees the rule of law. In the Federal Republic of Germany, Article 20, paragraph 3 of the constitution clearly spells out the principle and confirms that the state and all its subdivisions are subject to the law. Greatly inspired by the German principles, corresponding principles have been developed by the case law of the European Court of Justice, which has ruled a number of times on the actions of Community authorities.

The questions that need to be examined are whether and to what extent the rule of law, which has been so fundamental in the many decisions of the European Court of Justice, has had any noticeable impact in Belgium, both on the court system and in the legislature. In Belgium, the doctrine of legality ('l'Etat de droit'/'Rechtsstaat') has slowly developed under the influence of learned scholars and judges.[9] The doctrine of legality is also implicitly recognized by Articles 24, 67, 78, 92, 92, 106, 107 and 107ter of the Constitution. The principle that the state is subject to the law was first officially recognized in Belgium in ratifying the statutes of the Council of Europe,[10] which in Article 3 thereof confirms the principle of priority of the law and the bill of rights.

The doctrine of legality has mainly been seen in Belgium as the legal basis for asserting fundamental rights and liberties.[11] It has also been seen as the basic justification for preserving the separation of the three governmental powers – the legislature, the executive branch and the judiciary. In that sense, the rule of law has been seen in Belgium in a somewhat narrower sense than what the European Court of Justice has stated in a number of instances. At the European level, for instance, the separation of powers is not considered to be a prerequisite for establishing and preserving the rule of law.

However, it is difficult to see whether the principles of the rule of law as they are developed by the European Court of Justice have had any influence on Belgian jurisprudence and case law. The principle of the rule of law has developed in Belgium simultaneously with that of the Court of Justice, making it difficult to trace any direct relationship.

The European Court of Justice has developed in various rulings a set of rules around the doctrine of legality. A good example is the principle of protection of legitimate expectation or confidence which in turn came from the German concept of Vertrauenschutz. In the case III/63 *Lemmerz-Werke GmbH*, the European Court of Justice for the first time used the word 'Vertrauenschutz' and elaborated on the principle that Community subjects must have a legitimate confidence in the reliability of Community measures. The Court also often relies on the principle of no retroactivity of the law and on vested rights.[12] The European Court of Justice has also relied on the constitutional imperatives of legal certainty (sécurité juridique) and on the principle of proportionality (Verhältnismäszigkeit).

The principle of proportionality has been recognized in Community law in the case of 17 December 1970, *International Handelsgesellschaft gegen Einfuhr– und Vorratsstelle für Getreide– und Futtermittel*.[13] Its application shows great similarity to the German concept, according to which the Community may impose upon its citizens, in the interest of a public purpose, only such obligations and restrictions as are strictly necessary to attain that purpose.

Referring to Belgium, it is not obvious that these principles have influenced legal doctrine and case law. On the contrary, Belgian scholars have in recent years — as have court rulings — almost consistently deplored the decline of the rule of law in its recent developments in Belgium.[14] The criticism is generally viewed as a problem of society and generally focuses on the following trends: the growing complexity of the system of legal norms (directives, circulars, governmental pacts and declarations, etc.); the decline of the legislative function and the primacy of the executive; the increasing number of infringements on the separation of the powers principle; the violation of the principle of non-retroactivity of the law; and the increased discretionary power of the administration, in particular in the field of aid to enterprises.

This is not to suggest that Belgium might be worse off than the other Member States in the application of the rule of law. It suggests at least that the European Community has not exerted any noticeable influence — nor has it been a driving force — in the implementation of the rule of law in Belgium. On the other hand, we can certainly not infer that the European Community would have adversely influenced the Belgian legal system in the protection of the citizen under the rule of law.

Conclusion

The impact of Belgium's membership in the European Community on democracy in Belgium has been noticeable in two fields. First, the protection of fundamental rights by the European Convention, which is also a part of the law of the Community, as expressly referred to in the single European Act and other Community documents. The influence of the European Convention has been remarkable in many instances not only on the Belgian judiciary but also on Parliament and government. The evolution of the decisions of the Supreme Court has shown a clear trend in this respect. A number of changes in the laws and regulations have also been prompted by decisions of the Strasbourg Court.

Second, the influence has been noticeable with respect to the rule of law and due process. The European Community, in so far as it is based on the rule of law whereby Member States must determine whether measures adopted by them are in conformity with the basic constitutional charter, the Treaty, has introduced a new dimension in the Belgian framework of legal and political thinking: a greater awareness towards constitutionalism which has resulted in a limited judicial control of the constitutionality of laws. The awareness of the rule of law can also be traced in renewed procedures before the Council of State with respect to due process. Timid tendencies to improve due process in administrative proceedings are partly attributable to the EC's new awareness of due process.

Notes

1 *Official Journal* (1977) C. 103/1.
2 *Bulletin E.C.* (1978) 9, 3.
3 Solange I, 29 May 1974, BVerfGE 37, 271.
4 Avis du Conseil d'Etat sur le projet de loi portant approbation du traité créant la CED, *Doc. Parl.* Chambre, session 1952–1953, no. 163, 4, 5.
5 Article 140, paragraph 3, EEC Treaty.
6 Article 143, EEC Treaty.
7 Article 144, EEC Treaty.
8 Taquet, M. and C. Wantiez (1976) 'L'égalité des rémunérations des travailleurs masculins et féminins', *Journal des Tribunaux de Travail*, 137–43.
9 *Inter alia* Dumon, F. (1979–80) 'Over de Rechtsstaat', *Rechtskundig Weekblad*, 273–98, 337–68; Krings, E. (1989–90) 'Enkele beschouwingen betreffende rechtsstaat, scheiding der machten en rechterlijke macht', *Rechtskundig Weekblad*, 168–86.
10 Belgian law of 11 February 1950.
11 Krings, op. cit., 172.
12 Hubeau, Fr., Le Principe de la protection de la confiance légitime dans la jurisprudence de la Cour de Justice des Communautés Européennes, *Cahiers de Droit Europeen* 1983, 143–62.
13 *European Court Report* (1970) 1.125.
14 Quertainmont, P. (1984) 'Le Déclin de l'Etat de Droit', *Journal des Tribunaux*, 274 and 275; Krings, E., op. cit.

Chapter 13

The primacy of Community law

J.P. De Bandt

One of the most decisive changes in the Belgian legislative and judicial system has been the principle of the primacy of EC law. The objective of this chapter is to make a short cost-benefit analysis of the application of the principle of primacy by the Belgian Parliament, government and courts.

The primacy of Community law and its applicability

In the absence of any express provision in the Belgian constitution explicitly guaranteeing the primacy of Community law over conflicting national legislation, the influence of European Community law has culminated in a landmark decision of the Belgian Supreme Court of 27 May 1970. Before this decision, courts considered that a treaty approved by Parliament was legally equivalent to a law. In case of conflict between the treaty and the law, courts would apply the latest norm under the adagium 'lex posterior derogat legi priori'. This case law was dominated by a leading Supreme Court decision of 26 November 1925.

Much under the influence of the late General Public Prosecutor Hayoit de Termicourt, in his 'mercuriale' of 2 September 1963, and more decisively by his successor Ganshof van der Meersch, the principle of the primacy of rules of international law and Community law was introduced in the Belgian legal system through the above decision of the Belgian Supreme Court. Rules of international law or Community law, which are directly applicable, are to be applied by the Belgian courts notwithstanding the inconsistent provisions of national law. This principle applies both to the Community treaties and to the acts of the Community institutions.

In adopting this monistic approach, which was necessary in the absence of court control over the constitutionality of legislation acts, the Supreme Court provided a clear solution to guarantee the enforcement of the primacy of Community law. This rule is also clear when courts are called on to decide on national laws which violate Community law.

The rule also extends to courts holding inapplicable regional laws which violate Community law. Regional laws are laws enacted in Belgium by one of the three regions (the Flemish region, the Walloon region and the Brussels region) or by one of the three communities (the French community, the Flemish community and the German-speaking community) (NB: the Flemish region and the Flemish community have 'merged' into one entity, although they remain separate legal entities.)

Referring to the primacy rule with respect to the Belgian federalization process, the Court of Justice held that: 'important institutional reforms concerning the redistribution of powers and responsibilities between the national and regional institutions .. do not expunge the failure of the Kingdom of Belgium to fulfill its obligations'. According to established court case law, a Member State may not plead provisions, practices or circumstances in its internal legal system to justify failure to comply with obligations under Community law[1] (all concerning the non-implementation of EC directives on environmental policies).

The direct applicability of legal acts of Community institutions

One of the striking features of the European Community is the creation of a separate legal order and the direct applicability in the Member States of Community law and court decisions. This direct application in the Member States is the most revolutionary feature of the European construction which has had wide consequences in legislative and jurisdictional decision-making in the various Member States.

The principal legal instruments for the enactment and application of Community law are the acts of the Council and the Commission. A second group of legal instruments is formed by international treaties, conventions and agreements to which the Community is party. Regulations and directives are the most important of the legal acts of the Community. These important legislative acts have substantially modified the legislative work in the Member States and thus in Belgium.

The three characteristic elements of a Regulation are: (i) its general application; (ii) its binding character in all respects; and (iii) its direct applicability to each Member State. The general application of a regulation concerns the impersonal, non-individualized character of the situation to which it applies as well as the legal effects it entails for the legal subjects to whom it is addressed. A measure has general application provided 'it is applicable . . . to objectively determined situations and involves legal consequences for categories of persons viewed in a general and abstract manner'.[2]

A regulation not only has general application but is also binding in every respect. Moreover, a regulation is directly applicable to all Member States. Thus the Member States may not adopt measures applying the regulations which modify its scope or add provisions to it unless this is provided for in the regulation itself.[3] Both internal and external regulatory competence has, according to the case law of the Court, become the exclusive competence of the Community.

A directive has binding force in relation to the result to be achieved for each Member State to which it is addressed but it leaves the Member State free to choose the form of method for implementing it. As a rule, a directive is an instrument of Community intervention, often with a view to the harmonization of laws. Examples include food and drugs legislation, and indirect taxation. The Belgian legislator remains competent, for example, to regulate the right of establishment, but is obliged by Community law to remove legal provisions which discriminate against nationals of other EC countries. This has been done on various occasions.

As we can infer, these two legal instruments of Community institutions have had far-reaching consequences in the law-making process of the Member States. The effect is identical to all Member States, and, in that sense, Belgium has not reached different results than other Member States.

Another legal instrument is the decision. The decision is binding in all respects on its addressees. It can be addressed to Member States as well as to private parties and it is the means by which the Community adopts individual administrative acts. Decisions granting undertakings an exemption from the cartel prohibition, or decisions to abolish state aid, or decisions granting a negative clearance in competition matters are examples of administrative acts which can have wide-ranging consequences for a person or a company. This is another domain where administrative decisions have far-reaching effects in Member States. Many decisions have affected Belgian companies especially in the field of state aid and competition policy.

Conclusion

One of the main foundations on which the Court has built extensively is the principle of the supremacy of Community law which has had a direct influence on the Belgian legal scene. The principle has never been challenged by Belgian courts — unlike courts in some other Member States — and has become a cornerstone of the Belgian legal system. Curiously, however, this basic principle, which is also a principle of federal constitutionalism, has not been retained as a legal or constitutional principle in the various constitutional changes which Belgium has adopted since 1970 transforming the unitary system into a regional or semi-federal system.

Notes

1 Cases 68/81, 70/81, 72/81 and 73/81, Commission of the EC v. Kingdom of Belgium (1982) *European Court Report* 153, 163, 169, 175, 183, 189.
2 Case 6/68, Zuckerfabrik Watenstadt GmbH v. Council (1968), *European Court Report* 409 at 415.
3 Case 40/69, Hauptzollambt Hamburg-Oberelbe v. Firma Paul G. Bollmann (1970), *European Court Report* 69 at 79 (the 'turkey tail' case).

Chapter 14

The Belgian federalization process

J.P. De Bandt

The federalization process

It is difficult to measure the influence of the European construction on the Belgian federalization process which has been underway since 1970 and which has its roots in the early 1960s. During the past 20 years, Belgium has slowly evolved from being a centralized and unitary state in which language patterns had no particular political significance in the institutional framework to a state comprised of formally recognized language regions. Since Parliament's approval of the major language laws in 1962–3, Belgium has moved towards three major constitutional reforms: the first in 1970; the second in 1980; and the third, in 1988–9. The main features of the system as it stands today stem from the constitutional reform of 1970.

The constitutional reforms as a whole cannot be described in the scope of this analysis. Suffice to say that the broad lines of the restructuring is one which is featured solely along language lines. Four linguistic regions have been recognized: the Dutch language region, the French language region, the German language region, and the bilingual region of Brussels (3bis of the Constitution). In addition to the four language regions, three communities were created: the French community; the Flemish community; and the German-speaking community.

Communities do not correspond to the language regions referred to above. This is because Brussels is a linguistic region but not a community. This is one of the special features of the Belgian 'federal' system. Language regions do not correspond to communities, creating thereby a dichotomy between language regions, which create a territorial jurisdiction, and communities, which create a personal jurisdiction. The French community has jurisdiction over persons living in Walloonia, the Walloon institutions and the French-speaking institutions in Brussels. The Flemish community has jurisdiction over persons living in Flanders and the Flemish institutions in Brussels. The German-speaking community has jurisdiction over persons and institutions in the German-speaking territory in the east of Belgium.

The communities are competent in cultural matters, education, cultural cooperation, the use of language and so-called 'personalized matters' which are matters within the realm of personal life such as health-care, social and family policy.

Finally, in addition to the four language regions and the three communities, the constitutional reforms have organized three regions which are territorial entities: the Walloon region, the Flemish region and the Brussels region. These are political entities with essentially economic competences, including but not limited to environmental problems, regional aspects of credit policy, foreign trade, energy, public works and transport, urban planning, provincial and municipal institutions, scientific research and monuments and sites.

This is a second feature of the Belgian 'federal' construction; the regions correspond to neither the communities nor the language regions. The German community is enclosed in the Walloon region and the Flemish and the French community exercise their competence in the Brussels region. This Belgian model has often been referred to as a 'sui generis' model as opposed to the classical federal models such as the Federal Republic of Germany, Switzerland, the United States, Canada and others. As a result, we cannot trace any influence from the European Community on these constitutional changes.

Built on its own merits, the Belgian paradigm results from a long history made out of language conflicts between the two predominant language communities. Belgian constitutional reforms, which would probably have seen the light much earlier and certainly long before the signature of the Treaty of Rome, were substantially slowed down by the two world wars. We can therefore safely conclude that this vast state reform occurred independently of the European construction. The legislative history of the constitutional reform of 1970 even shows that the founding fathers did not intend to create a true federalist system. No studies, no plans, no blueprints of the federal Belgium were prepared. At the time Europe could hardly have served as a source of inspiration for Belgium. The pragmatic approach of the European founding fathers along the lines of the Monnet doctrine, as opposed to the Spinelli school of thought, was scarcely inhibited by federalist principles and could obviously not have exerted a strong influence on the building of any federal system in Europe. The discovery of federal principles, the rule of subsidiarity, and the federal institutional framework are recent trends within the European Commission's thinking, now repeatedly stressed by its president, Mr. J. Delors.

The various groups and organizations of European federalists in Belgium, which have been closer to the Spinelli line of thinking, have generally been very critical of Belgian constitutional reforms. Their criticism was aimed, in particular, at pointing out how much the Belgian reform was influenced by nationalistic ideologies which run counter to the move towards a unified federal Europe. Many scholars who witnessed the prevailing influence of Flemish and Walloon nationalisms in the basic architecture of the constitutional reform in 1970 also shared that criticism. In this sense, the Belgian devolution process towards two (or three) regions has been seen by some as the emergence of two new nation-states, again in total contradiction with the aims and objectives of the European Community.

We can conclude that the European federalist ideas have not exerted any influence on Belgian state reforms. The federalization process of the Belgian state should be seen as a devolution process which precedes – in terms of thinking and general framework – the Coal and Steel Community and the European Community.

Belgian influence

Assuming that the European community has not had any visible influence on the Belgian federalization process, the reverse is also true. Over the years, Belgium has exerted strong pressure on the Community in the building of a genuine European Community. This influence has been felt more in the field of economic and monetary union than in the field of institutions and political framework. Among the founders of the European Community, Belgium – and the Benelux countries as a whole – undoubtedly played a major role both at the time of the inception of the Community as in subsequent years. Statesmen such as Spaak, Van Zeeland and Snoy et d'Oppuers were leading inspirators in the early years (see also Chapter 11). Later, Belgium remained in favour of changes in the institutional structure of the Community in 1984–6 and was ready to accept a new European Act, as far reaching as that proposed in the Genscher-Colombo plan or the Spinelli initiatives.

More recently, however, scholars have deplored that the Belgian state reform and Belgian federalism in particular have not exerted more influence on the institutional structure of the Community. Belgium is ideally situated to show the European Community how to unite language diversity. A country in which the Latin and the German culture meet and in which three major languages of the Community are spoken, Belgium has a unique opportunity to pave the way for a workable federalist system which could serve as the model for the European Community. Thus far, however, not much inspiration has come from the Belgian model. As indicated above, the basic configuration of communities (personal jurisdiction) and overlapping regions (territorial jurisdiction) is one that could hardly be used in a broader European context.

The absence of the primacy rule – whereby federal law overrides regional or Community law in case of conflict – is another striking feature of the Belgian system, which contradicts the primacy rule inherent in all federal systems and which is already today one of the characteristics of the European Community: the primacy and direct applicability of Community law.

The regional dimension

Much emphasis has been placed in Belgium on an emerging Europe of regions, in which the Belgian regions would become a constituent part of federal Europe. The advocates in Belgium of a Europe of regions equivocally disregard the fact that Belgium is formed of Regions and Communities and that the Europe of regions would be composed of territorial entities only. They also underestimate the enduring role of the national states in the integration process. Yet the regional dimension of Europe has lately come to the forefront of discussions. A renewed interest in regions as separate components in the European construction is exerting influence on both the Flemish and the Walloon regions. Both regions have recently been enthusiastic supporters of 'l'Europe des Regions' and participate actively in the newly created influence of European regions. The pressure by the Flemish and Walloon regions in the European Community towards the recognition of regions is certainly one which will be felt in the future.

The new rule on equal treatment

In the recent state reform of 1988, one major — almost revolutionary — change was introduced; hopefully it will serve as a useful precedent at the level of the European Community. The change concerns Article 6 and 6bis of the Constitution, which confirms the principle of the equality of all Belgians and gives to any citizen a direct jurisdictional recourse to the Court of Arbitration for any violation of the principle of equality.

The first major decision of the Court of Arbitration indicated that this basic right will receive extensive protection. Many constitutionalists see it as a major breakthrough in the protection of the bill of rights. Hopefully this principle of direct recourse to the Court of Arbitration might be of interest in the European Community.

'Federal loyalty'

One principle of EC law has noticeably influenced Belgian public law, in particular, within the scope of the Belgian federalization process under the successive state reforms. It is the principle of federal loyalty which, in turn, has deep roots in the federal system of the Federal Republic of

Germany, the so-called 'Bundestreue'. Federal loyalty is based on the idea that in a federal state, all component units of the state must abide by the division of competences among the various levels of government and must collaborate and cooperate effectively among them.

There are basically three elements in the federal loyalty principle: first, the obligation for the state or a sub-division of the state to perform correctly under the obligation set forth by law and not to make an abusive usage of its own competences; second, the obligation to cooperate actively and loyally in the realization of the objectives described in the treaties; and finally, an obligation of solidarity within the framework of Community objectives.

The European Court of Justice held the principle of EC federal loyalty to be a legally binding principle and not merely a policy objective. This principle has to be seen as a separate source of law, thereby creating rights and obligations for the parties (Court of Justice, 21 February 1987, Case 186/85, *Commission v. Belgium*, 1987, ECR 2029). It also means that all Member States and their sub-divisions are to abide by this loyalty principle within the scope of their respective competences.

The federal loyalty principle, therefore, is to be applied at the following levels: between the Community and the Member States, between Member States, and between Community institutions. The most express reference to the loyalty principle is to be found in Article 5 of the Treaty of Rome, which states:

> Member States shall take all appropriate measures, whether general or particular, to ensure fulfilment of the obligations arising out of this Treaty or resulting from action taken by the institutions of the Community. They shall facilitate the achievement of the Community's tasks.

Article 5 is, no doubt, the most obvious reference to the loyalty principle. Other provisions bear on the same issue. Article 38, paragraph 4, of the Treaty, for instance, provides that:

> The operation and development of the common market for agricultural products must be accompanied by the establishment of a common agricultural policy among the Member States.

Other provisions call for active and loyal cooperation between the Community and Member States. Article 6, for instance, provides that:

1. Member States shall, in close cooperation with the institutions of the Community, coordinate their respective economic policies to the extent necessary to attain the objectives of this Treaty.
2. The institutions of the Community shall take care not to prejudice the internal and external financial stability of the Member States.

Collaboration is also called for in articles 102A, 103, 104, 107 and 109 of the Treaty. The obligation of solidarity is described in article 108, paragraph 2, of the Treaty. The Court of Justice has mainly stressed, in a number of decisions, the importance of loyalty in the relationship between the Community and Member States. Less case law is to be found where the loyalty obligation between Member States is taken into account.

Between Community institutions, however, there is not yet anything like the German concept of 'Organtreue' which is noticeable. We can nevertheless expect that within the framework of the Single Act and the reinforcement of the role of the parliament (Article 100A and Article 149 of the Treaty), the principle of federal loyalty will also develop in the relationship between Community institutions. The principle of federal loyalty, which carries so much weight at Community level, has exerted considerable influence on Belgian scholars who are actively engaged in framing new principles of Belgian federal law.[1]

Scholars insist that the loyalty principle be taken up as a guiding principle of Belgian federal law. Suggestions have even be made that the principle be included as a constitutional provision in the sense of Article 5 of the Treaty of Rome which can be tested and challenged before the Arbitration Court.[2] Although the principle of loyalty finds most of its usefulness in a vertical division of competences and in a system where the primary rule is in effect, most Belgian authors nonetheless believe that the principle of loyalty finds a strong base in the Belgian system, where there is no hierarchy of legal norms, and hence no primacy of a national federal law, and where a division of competences is, in principle, based on exclusivity.

Federal loyalty is all the more needed because Belgium is going through a devolution process from a unitary centralized state to a regional system. Belgium is undergoing a centrifugal movement compared to Europe which, on the contrary, moves towards more unity and is thus a centripetal model. The federal loyalty principle has thus far not yet been tested before the Court of Arbitration, the Council of State or other courts. In one case, the Court of Arbitration, dealing with regional taxes, has indirectly alluded to the obligation of the regions to abide by the guiding principles of the economic and monetary union.[3] However, the principle of federal loyalty, inspired largely by principles laid down by the European Court of Justice, will probably continue to influence Belgian decision-makers and courts in the years to come.

We should observe that the Council of State, in its advisory function, has on several occasions insisted on the necessity of cooperation among the various components of the federal state. Autonomy of these components, the cornerstone of the system, does not mean, according to several opinions rendered by the Council of State, that these component parts of the new federal state should not seek to cooperate actively.[4]

Conclusion

The European Community has not exerted any influence on the Belgian federalization process. The two processes are very different in nature. Belgium is evolving from a unitary state toward a federal state, which implies a devolution of powers from the centre toward the regions. European integration is an opposite movement whereby national competences are transferred to the Community. Historically too the Belgian devolution process, which started in 1970, is based on institutional blueprints which precede the signing of the Treaty of Rome. The underlying philosophy of the Belgian reforms, which was aimed primarily at resolving a nationality problem and at recognizing and institutionalizing the right and existence of nations is a long way from the dominant European federalist thinking, which focuses more on diversity, a bill of rights, and the gradual disappearance of the nation-state.

Notes

1 See in this respect van Gerven, W., en Gilliams, H., 'Gemeenschapstrouw: goede trouw' in E.G.-Verband, *Rechtskundig Weekblad*, 1989–90, 1160; see in particular Alen, A., en Peeters, P., 'Bundestreue' in het Belgisch grondwettelijk recht, *Rechtskundig Weekblad*, 1989–90, 1122; Alen, A., en Peeters, P., 'Samenwerkingsverbanden tussen de Staat, de Gemeenschappen en de Gewesten', in *Staat, Gemeenschappen en Gewesten*, Die Keure, 1989; Alen, A., en Peeters, P., 'België op zoek naar een cooperatief staatsmodel', *Tijolschrift voor Bestuurswetenschappen en Publick Recht*, 1989.

2 van Gerven and Gilliams, *op. cit.* p. 1167.

3 Arbitragehof, Judgment no. 47, 25 February 1988.

4 *Official Gazette*, 17 March 1988. For a detailed description of these opinions of the Council of State see Alen, A., en Peeters, P., ibid. 1150 et seq.

PART IV: SOCIAL AND CULTURAL POLICIES

Chapter 15

Labour migration

Filip Abraham

In the discussion on 1992, considerable attention is being paid to the free movement of labour within the EC. Although the freedom of labour movements is guaranteed by the EC Treaty, many observers feel that, until now, the EC has failed in this respect. It is argued that this lack of intra-EC labour mobility hampers to an important degree the efficient allocation of resources.

In this chapter, we analyse the validity of this argument for Belgium. We argue that although the impact of the EC on labour migration into and out of Belgium has indeed been limited, this does not imply that the EC has failed to achieve an efficient resource allocation. In fact, the strong trade expansion that followed the creation of the EC involved a large indirect exchange of labour services, which replaced the direct transfer of labour that might otherwise have taken place. In short, trade in goods was substituted for trade in labour.

This simple point is made in the following steps. First we focus on the impact of the EC on labour migration in the case of Belgium. We briefly summarize EC regulations on labour migration and some figures and studies on labour migration in Belgium are presented. We then discuss the role of international trade as a substitute for international labour mobility. Finally, we offer some concluding comments.

International labour migration

EC regulations on labour migration

Free migration of labour within the EC is guaranteed by Article 7 of the EC Treaty, which forbids discrimination because of nationality. Articles 48 and following apply this principle to the case of labour mobility and employment. Such freedom of movement entails the abolition of any discrimination based on nationality between workers of the Member States as regards employment, remuneration and other conditions of

Table 15.1 *Foreign employees in Belgium and Belgian employees in the EC, 1985*

Foreign employees in Belgium	
Total number of foreign employees	187,000
Foreign employees as % of total employees	6.2
EC nationals in total foreign employees (%)	75.2
Foreign employees from each member country in the total of EC employees (%)	
Denmark	0.5
Germany	4.3
Greece	2.8
Spain	10.9
France	17.1
Ireland	0.4
Italy	43.5
Luxembourg	0.9
Netherlands	12.8
Portugal	2.5
United Kingdom	4.4
Nationals of non-EC countries in total foreign employees (%)	24.8

Belgian employees in the EC	
Total number of Belgian employees in other EC countries excluding Spain and Italy*	54,500
Belgian employees in each member country as % of total migrants in EC excluding Spain and Italy*	
Denmark	0.2
Germany	13.2
Greece	0.4
Spain	n.a.
France	22.8
Ireland	0.0
Italy	n.a.
Luxemburg	16.7
Netherlands	40.4
Portugal	0.4
United Kingdom	6.1

*: Data are not available.
n.a. = Figures are not available.

Source: Eurostat (1989) *Employment and Unemployment*, Luxemburg.

work and employment. Self-employed and independent persons are given comparable rights, with the exception of the public sector and activities which are connected, even occasionally, with the exercise of official authority (Article 55). Numerous directives and decisions by the Court of Justice have applied the principle of free labour movement within the EC in practice. No such rights are automatically granted to nationals on non-Member States.

Some facts for Belgium

Table 15.1 presents some data on labour migration into and out of Belgium. In 1985, 187,000 foreign employees worked in Belgium of whom 75.2 per cent were nationals of other EC countries. When related to the total labour force, the share of foreign employees remains limited (6.2 per cent). In view of this fact, we can safely say that the creation of the EC has not led to a substantial labour inflow in Belgium.

This conclusion is reinforced when we consider that 43.5 per cent of EC workers in Belgium have Italian nationality. A large share of these workers moved to Belgium in the 1950s before the EC was formed. Similarly, most of the immigration from Spain, Portugal and Greece, occurred before the entry of these countries to the EC. Furthermore, some of the German, Dutch and French workers in Belgium reside in their country of origin. It is not clear whether such 'border trade' would not have taken place without the EC. Finally, it should be noted that 24.8 per cent of foreign employees come from non-member countries and thus do not benefit from EC regulations on labour mobility.

A similar picture emerges from the data on Belgians working in other EC countries. With only 54,500 Belgian workers in other EC countries, excluding Spain and Italy, Belgium was a net importer of labour from the EC in 1985. Virtually all of these workers found a job in the neighbouring countries of The Netherlands, France, Germany and Luxemburg. Presumably, some of these workers live in Belgium close to the borders. As mentioned earlier, the impact of the EC on this type of labour migration is hard to determine.

While the share of foreign workers in the Belgian work-force is limited, their impact on production and employment in specific sectors may be significant. Table 15.2 indicates that in 1985, foreign employment accounted for 10 per cent or more of total employment in Energy and water, Mineral extraction and chemicals, Metal manufacturing and engineering, and Construction. Moulaert (1978) uses the 1970 input—output table to estimate the effects of a reduction of foreign employment by 1000 workers in two of these industries. In 1970, such reduction in the Belgian construction industry implied a decline of foreign employment by 3.75 per cent. From his simulations, Moulaert concludes that production in the construction industry would fall by 2.52 per cent. A similar experiment for the Metal manufacturing sector would lead to a supply contraction of 6.1 per cent in that industry. Through forward and backward linkages, other sectors would also be significantly affected. Here, the estimated employment and production losses appear unexpectedly high, presumably because of the author's assumption that Belgians do not replace foreign workers and that the production technology remains unchanged. We also wonder how evolution in the 1980s would compare with Moulaert's results. Unfortunately, no update of his study is available.

Table 15.2 *Sectoral disaggregation of foreign workers in Belgium (% share of foreign employees in total employment by industry: 1985)*

Agriculture, forestry and fishing	6.7
Energy and water	11.8
Mineral extraction and chemicals	13.2
Metal manufac. and engineering	10.0
Other manufac. industries	6.6
Construction and civil engineering	10.6
Distributive trade, etc.	8.6
Transport and communications	2.9
Financing, insurance, etc.	5.6
Other services	3.2
Total	6.2

Source: Eurostat (1989) *Employment and Unemployment*, Luxemburg.

Foreign trade as indirect international labour migration

The absence of large labour movements among EC countries does not imply that the EC has failed to exploit the gains of international migration. In the light of the substantial trade expansion (see Chapter 8), part of which is generally attributed to the creation of the EC, it appears that international trade rather than labour migration has narrowed the differences in labour productivity between EC Member States. In other words, trade in goods has replaced trade in labour.

The result that international trade acts as a substitute for international factor mobility is well-known from international trade theory. If barriers or mobility costs impede factor movements, countries export factor services instead of the factors themselves. Export specialization takes place in goods which intensively use the country's cheap production factors. *Ceteris paribus*, goods are exported in the production process of which an efficient use of labour creates a cost advantage *vis-à-vis* the trading partners. Similarly, products are imported that, given the factor prices in the home country, entail a more expensive production process. This exchange of labour services through exports and imports gives trading countries the benefits of a more cost-effective use of domestic and foreign labour without any actual transfer of labour. Furthermore, it puts downward pressure on the prices of factors that are more expensive in the home country than in other countries. Applied to labour, this means that international wage differentials are reduced and, in the extreme case even eliminated, as a consequence of international trade. In this way, international trade achieves similar results to international labour migration.

The transfer of labour services included in Belgian foreign trade can be measured by computing the labour content of exports and imports. Based on an input–output methodology, Peeters and Van Heden (1981a and b) compute the employment effects of an expansion of Belgian exports to and imports from the EC.

Their findings suggest that trade expansion with EC Member States contained a large exchange of labour services, reducing the need for international labour migration (although we can only guess what would have happened without the creation of the EC). In addition, Belgium substantially benefited from the EC. It exported more labour services than it imported. We can safely say that at least some of the workers who found a job in the export industries would have been unemployed or would have been forced to migrate.

Yet international trade also imposes *costs on labour in the form of enhanced intersectoral labour mobility*. Instead of moving abroad, workers have to reallocate from contracting import-competing to expanding export industries.

Conclusion

In this chapter, we have analysed the impact of the EC on labour migration in the case of Belgium. While the EC treaty guarantees free international labour mobility, the role of foreign employees in the Belgian labour force remains limited, although their impact on some sectors may be important. Even then, most of the migration into Belgium cannot be attributed to the creation of the EC. Migration of Belgians to other EC countries is even smaller, so that Belgium is a net importer of labour with regard to the EC.

The absence of large labour movements between EC countries is partially explained by the strong trade expansion as a result of trade liberalization. Trade of goods implies an indirect exchange of labour services. Studies for Belgium indicate that this indirect transfer of labour was substantial. This substitution of international trade for direct labour export was beneficial for the Belgian economy, as it reaped the benefits of a better international resource allocation without the production factors actually moving abroad. At the same time, mobility costs in the form of intersectoral reallocation were imposed on labour.

Where does that leave us in the coming years? The renewed effort towards market integration is revitalizing trade among EC countries and therefore reinforce the indirect exchange of labour services. At the same time, the EC promotes international labour mobility through measures such as the mutual recognition of degrees. If this policy is successful it will probably generate greater international mobility of skilled labour between Belgium and its immediate neighbours. Increased labour mobility may also stimulate the incentives of less-skilled labour of southern EC countries to migrate to Belgium. Nevertheless, such evolution appears rather unlikely in the light of current attitudes towards migrant workers.

References

Eurostat (1988) Employment and Unemployment, Theme 3, Series C. Luxemburg.

Moulaert, F. (1978) 'The Structural Significance of Foreign Employment for the Belgian Economy: An Input–Output Analysis of Remigration Policy in Two Branches of the Belgian Economy', KUL, CES Regional Science Research Paper no. 20.

Peeters, T. and L. Van Heden (1981) 'Internationale Arbeidsverdeling en Herstructureringsproblemen in België', KUL, CES Working Paper 1981/03.

Van Heden, L. and T. Peeters (1981) 'Tewerkstellingsverschuivingen in België: Rationalisatie- en Herstructureringsproblemen 1965–1975', KUL, CES Working Paper, 1981/16.

Chapter 16

Labour relations

Roger Blanpain

Industrial relations and labour law vary widely between the different member countries of the EEC and this is probably going to stay this way for the years to come. One reason is that the necessary political will to develop a genuine European industrial relations and labour law system is at present lacking. Another is that trade unions and employers associations were and are fundamentally split on the idea of European labour law and European collective bargaining. Both concerns have been written right into the Single Act, which provides that the Council of Ministers has to decide unanimously on matters relating to the rights and interests of workers, which means that every country enjoys a right of veto. Exceptions are made for health and safety in the workplace where decisions can be taken by way of qualified majority.

The above mentioned reasons have had as a consequence that labour law and industrial relations have remained, up to now, rather national and the European impact, although important, remains legally and technically speaking rather marginal. We do not discuss here the different proposals which lay for years on the table, like the Vredeling proposals on information and consultation regarding the international enterprises, nor the proposed Vth directive on, among others, worker participation, nor the European Company Statute, which have not yet become Community law. We only consider those measures which have been translated into national law, with the exception of the last point, concerning the social charter, as this may relaunch the social debate in Europe and foster a more genuine social cohesion and dimension.

The following main points will be discussed:

- the free movement of labour
- the restructuring of enterprises
- the equal treatment of men and women
- the health and safety
- the solemn declaration of fundamental social rights: the Social Charter

The free movement of labour

Article 48 of the EEC treaty guarantees the freedom of 'workers' to accept firm offers of employment and to remain in a Member State for the purposes of carrying it out. Belgian legislation was fundamentally changed through the EEC regulation no. 1612/68 of 15 October 1968, so that neither limitation nor conditions could be imposed regarding employment of EEC nationals in Belgium. The Belgian rules concerning an EEC labour card became superfluous. The legislation now regarding employment of foreign workers, namely the Royal Decree of 20 July 1967, only applies to foreigners who are not EEC nationals, as EEC nationals enjoy freedom of movement.

On a number of occasions, however, Belgium has been summoned by the Commission before the European Court for not living up to Community standards. Those cases referred to the exception to free movement of labour for reasons of employment in the public service or for reasons of public policy, public security or public health.

Article 48(4) indeed provides an exception to the free movement of labour, namely in the case of employment in the public service. Belgian authorities had reserved posts for Belgians only as trainee locomotive drivers, loaders, plate-layers, shunters and signallers with the national railways and unskilled workers with the local railways as well as posts for hospital nurses, children's nurses, night-watchmen, plumbers, carpenters, electricians, architects, and supervisors with the City of Brussels and the Commune of Auderghem, and thus put restrictions on the free movement of labour. Belgium was asked by the Court of Justice to re-examine the issue and was finally condemned. The Court was of the opinion that the provision of Article 48(4) removes from the ambit of free movement of labour a series of posts which involve direct or indirect participation in the exercise of powers conferred by public law and duties designed to safeguard the general interests of the state or of other public authorities. Such posts in fact presume on the part of those occupying them the existence of a special relationship of allegiance to the state and reciprocity of rights and duties which form the foundation of the bond of nationality. The jobs reserved by the Belgian authorities did not meet those qualifications (*Commission of the European Communities v. Kingdom of Belgium*, Case 149/79, 17 December 1980, IELL, Case Law, 1 A, case no. 39 and case no. 149/79, 26 May 1982, ibid. no. 47).

In another case an action was initiated against the Belgian state by French plaintiffs in connection with the refusal by the administrative authority to issue a permit enabling them to reside in Belgian territory, on the grounds that their conduct was considered to be contrary to public policy by virtue that they were waitresses in a bar which was suspect from the moral point of view. The Belgian law of 21 August 1948 terminating official regulation of prostitution prohibits soliciting, incitement to debauchery, exploitation of prostitution, the keeping of a disorderly house or brothel or living on immoral earnings. Thus prostitution *per se* is not prohibited and does not give rise to repressive measures. In this case the European Court decided that a Member State may not, by virtue of the reservation relating to public policy contained in Article 48 of the Treaty, expel a national of another Member State from its territory or refuse him access to its territory by reason of conduct which, when attributable to the former state's own nationals, does not give rise to repressive measures or other genuine and effective measures intended to combat such conduct (*Rezguis Adoui v. Belgian State and City of Liège*, Cases 115 and 116/81, 18 May 1982), IELL, Case Law, 1 A, case no. 46). So in this case a permit had to be given by the Belgian authorities.

The restructuring of enterprises

Under this heading we have to consider the impact of the directives on *collective redundancies* (EEC/75/129 of 17 February 1975), on the safeguarding of employees' rights in the events of *transfers of undertakings, businesses or part of businesses* (EEC/77/187 of 14 February 1977) and on the protection of employees in the event of the *insolvency* of their employer (EEC/80/987 of 20 October 1980 and 87/164, 2 March 1987). These directives have been implemented by a number of measures in Belgium.

On 2 October 1975, the National Labour Council concluded an interindustrywide collective bargaining agreement in execution of the European directive of 17 February 1975, concerning the approximation of legislation regarding collective dismissals. 'Collective dismissals' means dismissals by an employer for one or more reasons not related to the individual workers concerned where over a period of 60 days the number of redundancies is:

1 at least 10 per cent in enterprises which, during the calendar year preceding the redundancies, on average employ more than 20 and less than 100 employees;
2 at least 20 per cent of the number of workers in enterprises which, during the calendar year preceding the redundancies, employ at least 100 but less than 300 workers;
3 at least 30 per cent in enterprises which, during the calendar year preceding the redundancies, employ on average at least 300 employees.

The agreement applies to 'technical units', in the sense of Article 14 of the act of 20 September 1948 concerning the organization of the economy, which employed on average more than 20 employees during the year before the dismissals. The employer who finds he has to dismiss his employees collectively must *inform* and *consult the employees* as indicated in collective bargaining agreement no. 9 of March 1972. In the absence of a works' council or a union delegation, the employer will inform and consult with the employees themselves or with their representatives. The consultation will cover the possibility of avoiding or limiting the dismissals, as well as the possibility of mitigating their consequences. To this end the employer must give the employees' representatives the necessary information and provide in writing the reasons for the dismissals, the number of employees to be dismissed, the average number of employees occupied in the enterprise and the date on which the dismissals will take place. This information enables the employees' representatives to formulate observations and suggestions.

The Royal Decree of 24 May 1976 provides that the employer who envisages a collective dismissal is obliged to send a copy of this information to the director of the regional office of the State Employment Agency. He must also give the director, by registered letter, the following information: the name and address of the enterprise; the nature of the activity carried out by the enterprise; the number of employees who work there; the reasons for the job qualifications and position in the enterprise and the consultations which have taken place in conformity with the collective agreement mentioned above. The employer is not allowed to dismiss the employees before a period of 30 days has elapsed, which commences on the day on which the regional director is notified. The director can extend this period to 60 days. In that case the employer must be informed at least a week before the first period of 30 days has expired. The employer can appeal against the director's decision to the governing body of the State Employment Agency, which will decide within a period of 30 days. An appeal does not suspend the decision. The Royal Decree of 1976 also applies to a closure of an enterprise, which is not the consequence of a judicial decision.

Enterprises which employ, on average, 50 or more employees are, in accordance with inter-industrywide collective agreement no. 27 concluded in the National Labour Council, obliged to inform the works' council or the union delegation immediately when there has been a delay of more than three months in the payment of the official social security contribution to the National Insurance Service, or in the payment of fiscal contributions or value added tax to the Department of Finance. The employer also has the duty to inform the 'Office for Enterprises in Difficulties', which was set up by the Department of Economic Affairs.

In execution of a European Directive of 14 February 1977 on the harmonization of employees' rights in the case of transfers of undertakings, businesses or parts of businesses, Belgium now has specific provisions protecting the acquired rights of the employee in the case of the transfer of an enterprise, or part of an enterprise, pursuant to an agreement, to a new employer; as a result of, for example, a merger, cession, absorption or amalgamation. A mere economic concentration which leaves the legal personality of the employer unchanged (for example, the sale of shares is not sufficient). These provisions are laid down in an inter-industrywide collective agreement No. 32bis concluded in the National Labour

Council on 7 June 1985. This agreement provides for the automatic transfer of the individual employment relationship, and the rights and duties which go along with it, to the new employer; an exception is made for the rights of the employees relating to pension schemes and invalidity provisions, which are complementary to the advantages given within the framework of the official social security system.

The transfer does not itself constitute a reason, either for the transferor or for the acquirer (the new employer), to dismiss the employee. Transferred employees can, however, be dismissed for just cause or for reasons of an economic, technical or organizational nature. This means that the principle of automatic transfer of the employment relationship in the case of transfer has been relieved of any real content; the new employer also has the legal right to renegotiate the wages and conditions of employment of transferred employees after the transfer has taken place. Employees who are taken over by a new employer, however, do continue to enjoy their full seniority with regard to the length of notice which the new employer will have to respect in the case of dismissal.

In the case of the transfer of enterprises, the subject of a bankruptcy or a judicial agreement, specific rules apply. There is no automatic transfer of acquired rights. If the transfer of the enterprise is realized within a period of six months after the bankruptcy, the new employer can choose the employees he wants to hire. For those workers who are engaged, the collective agreed-upon working conditions and job classification remains valid. The seniority acquired with the former employer and the period between bankruptcy and his engagement as well as the seniority with the new employer are all taken into account for the calculation of the term of notice, in case the employee would be dismissed, with the exception however of dismissal during the trial period (with the new employer).

By the Act of 30 June 1967 the Fund available for the compensation of employees who are dismissed when an enterprise closes down was also charged with the payment of remuneration and compensation for lack of notice if the employer failed to make these payments to his workers when an enterprise was being closed down. The 1967 Act applies to all enterprises, regardless of how many employees they employed. Employees who are not taken over in the event of a takeover, and who are not paid by their (former) employer, may also benefit from payments made by the Fund. All employees can benefit from the activities of the Fund, whatever the length of their seniority or whatever kind of labour contract they have. Even an employee who is dismissed for just cause can claim from the Fund. However, there is a maximum the employee can obtain: namely 900,000 Belgian francs. The Fund will, *de jure*, put forward the rights and claims of the employee in order to recoup the payments from the employer. The Fund is a privileged creditor if the employer fails or becomes insolvent.[1]

The equal treatment of men and women

The equal treatment of men and women (see also Chapter 13) has been one of the most important and relatively successful areas of social intervention by the European Communities.[2] In this context reference has to be made to Article 119 of the Treaty, the *Equal Pay* directive (no. 75/117 of 10 February 1975), and the directive concerning *equal treatment for men and women as regards access to employment, vocational training and promotion, and working conditions* (no. 76/207), 9 February 1976).

The principle of equal pay for equal work is not only laid down in Article 119 (a self-executing article) of the Treaty of Rome which created the European Economic Community; but it is also provided for in Article 47bis of the Act of 12 April 1965 on the protection of remuneration. Article 47bis makes it legally possible for the employee to go to court if the principle of equal pay has not been respected. This right has not in fact been used, for reasons which are self-evident: it is almost impossible for the employee to sue his employer during the existence of the employment relationship for numerous reasons including fear of reprisals, the time-consuming nature of the procedure, the fact that his wages are negotiated by the unions who should help him with legal aid and thus, in reality, sue themselves and so on.

A European directive on equal pay enacted on 10 February 1975 gave birth to an inter-industrywide collective agreement which was concluded in the National Labour Council on 25 October 1975 (no. 25). This agreement contains the principle of equal pay for equal work, or for work of equal value. Discrimination based on sex is forbidden, and the agreement also lays down that the criteria used to draw up the job classification must not be discriminatory either. The employee can complain to the Labour Court if he thinks that he is being discriminated against. The Court can then appoint an *ad hoc* committee, jointly composed of trade union and employers' association representatives, and ask for its advice. When an employee files a grievance, informs the union delegation or the labour inspectorate, or sues in the Labour Court because he feels that he has been discriminated against in the field of equal pay, the employer must not retaliate by dismissing him or changing the conditions of his work. If the employer does this, he will have to prove that his decision to dismiss the worker or to change his working conditions was based on other grounds; and if he fails to prove this, the employee can request reinstatement or a return to previous working conditions. If the employer does not agree to reinstatement, the employee is entitled to an indemnification equal to six months wages or to a sum equal to the real damages he is able to prove.

Title V of the Act of 4 August 1978 on economic reorientation implements the directive of the European Council of Ministers of 9 February 1976 on the implementation of the principle of equal treatment for men and women as regards access to employment, vocational training, promotion and working conditions. It reads: 'equal treatment of men and women regarding working conditions, access to employment, vocational training, promotion and access to self employment' and is, as indicated, of European inspiration. This 1978 Act has consequently to be studied in conjunction with Article 119 of the EEC treaty concerning equal pay for equal work and the directive of 10 February 1975 on the approximation of the laws of the Member States relating to the application of the principle of equal pay for men and women.

The Belgian government declared at the time of the adoption of the Act that: 'No action aimed at equalizing the chances and treatment of female employees should depart from the fundamental principle that each human being, whether a man or a woman, has the undeniable right to work'. The Act is of public order, which means that stipulations or practices contrary to the Act are absolutely null and void. It covers the public as well as the private sector.

Article 118 of the 1978 Act prohibits 'every form of discrimination on the grounds of sex, either directly or indirectly by referring to marital status or family situation'. Article 118 thus prohibits direct discrimination and, in certain circumstances, indirect discrimination. This means that the application of equal conditions, which may have a discriminatory effect due to the situation prevalent in one of the categories, can in itself be discriminatory. An example would be the fixing of a maximum age for starting a certain job which may discriminatorily disqualify women who did not wish to enter the labour force during the period they were bearing and raising their children. The intentions of the employer are not relevant: whether he wants to discriminate or not is not the point. Only the consequences of his behaviour are to be taken into account. If they result in discriminatory treatment, this is sufficient to be contrary to the law. Equal treatment must be guaranteed in relation to access to employment, promotion, vocational training, self-employment, working conditions and the annual vacation.

Not only 'stipulations' but also 'practices' contrary to the Act are null and void. 'Stipulations' are: 'the legal and administrative rules, the individual labour contracts and collective labour agreements, work rules . . .'; 'practices' are: 'each individual or repeated act by a public or a private institution, by an employer or a person, effectuated to another person or a group of persons. . .'. Equality should prevail just as much with regard to promotion as with regard to access to a job, whatever the job or its hierarchical position. The same conditions and selection procedure, selection criteria included, should apply. The Act explicitly forbids any reference to the sex of an employee in job announcements or in advertisements for jobs or promotion; even indirect indications are illegal. Direct or indirect references to sex relating to the hiring conditions, selection criteria or the selection itself are also illegal, as is the actual barring of access to a job or to promotion on the grounds of sex.

Equal treatment applies to vocational training, vocational information, apprenticeship, adult education and social promotion, both in the public and in the private sector; equal treatment should also be guaranteed regarding participation in examinations and conditions for the granting and award of all sorts of diplomas, certificates and titles. Any references to sex in conditions or criteria are forbidden in this area too. Equal treatment does not apply to education in general, and does not lead — at least in the immediate future — to mixed vocational schools, although this is an unspoken aim. It was agreed in parliament that every child, be it a boy or a girl, should have — within a given region — the chance to enrol in any training programme. The Minister of Employment and Labour has been charged to see to the implementation of this policy.

Wages and working conditions in the broadest sense should also be equal. This includes, *inter alia*, stipulations and practices relating to:

- the individual labour contract
- apprenticeship
- collective agreements
- working time and working time arrangements (e.g. flexi-time)
- holidays
- Sunday rest
- work rules
- health and safety of employees
- employment of young people
- works councils, committees for safety, health and embellishment, union delegations
- the promotion of labour and the improvement of the working life
- wages and their protection
- credit hours and indemnification for social promotion
- annual vacation
- practices relating to the physical, moral or psychological working conditions (work rhythm and tempo).

The 1978 Act providing for equal treatment contains a number of exceptions:

- *Protection of motherhood*, covering pregnancy and maternity.
- *Positive discrimination*: what is meant by this are measures which in fact discriminate but which really promote equal opportunity for men and women, in particular by removing existing inequalities which affect women's opportunities. The Executive will indicate these 'exceptional' measures after consultation with the National Women's Council and the National Labour Council. In this area we may foresee special training programmes; we could also imagine the employment of a certain number of women being made a condition for obtaining government contracts, or the imposition of goals or even quotas. However, it is not very likely that the Belgian government will

embark within the near future on the road of goals and quotas.

- Equal treatment does not exclude the possibility of determining, exceptionally, *occupational activities* for which, by reason of their nature or the context in which they are carried out, the sex of the worker continues to be a determining factor. In conformity with the 1976 directive the Belgian government abolished a number of prohibited tasks, such as certain painting jobs and work involving heavy loads.
- Unequal treatment regarding *underground labour* and hazardous and unhealthy work is provisionally regarded as compatible with the equal treatment provisions. In conformity with the 1976 directive the Belgian government will carry out an examination and, if necessary, abolish the relevant laws or regulations within a period of four years of notification of the directive.
- The same goes for rules concerning *night work* and certain specific provisions in the General Regulation for Labour Protection (separate facilities and the like).

For the enforcement of the equal treatment provisions the Belgian legislature relies in the first place on the normal social inspectorate and then on penal sanctions. Stipulations and practices contrary to the equal treatment provisions are null and void, and anyone who suffers any prejudice can sue before the competent court in order to obtain the implementation of the law. The trade unions are given the legal capacity to sue in all litigation arising from the application of the Act in defence of the interest of their members. This representation by an organization does not affect the right of members to bring an action individually or to intervene therein at any stage.

Normally the courts will only grant compensation — not instatement or reinstatement, for example — in the case of discrimination, and it is up to the applicant or to the employee to prove that he or she is being discriminated against, as well as proving the amount of damage suffered. The court can, on its own initiative, order the employer to stop discriminatory practices relating to vocational training, working conditions and conditions or criteria for dismissal, under the threat of penal sanctions. The 1978 Act also foresees specific measures to protect the employee against retaliation from the employer as a reaction to a complaint within the undertaking or to any legal proceedings aimed at enforcing compliance with the principle of equal treatment. In the case of a complaint or legal action by the employee the employer is not allowed to change his working conditions unilaterally or to dismiss him, except for reasons which have nothing to do with the complaint or the legal action. The burden of proof is reversed, and if the employer cannot prove his point and is not willing to reintegrate the employee, then additional compensation, equal to six months remuneration, is due unless the employee can prove that his damages should be even higher.

A number of Belgian cases before the European Court were allowed to elaborate on a number of concepts involved in the implementation of the principle of equal treatment. The most important are the *Defrenne* (an air-hostess, employed by Sabena) *cases* which related to the notion of pay, the self-executing character of Article 119 of the Treaty and working conditions (the moment at which the labour contract takes an end (*Gabrielle Defrenne v. Belgian State*, Case 80/70, 25 May 1971, IELL; idem, no. 4; *v. Sabena*, Case 43/75, 8 April 1976; ibid. no. 22 and Case 149/77, 15 June 1978).

Health and safety

Quite a number of measures have been taken by the EEC in the area of health and safety and, as indicated above, they can be taken by way of qualified majority by the Council of Ministers. Among the most important are the *framework directive* of 12 June 1989 and other directives, which have been accepted or are in the pipeline: *work places, work equipment, personnel protective equipment, work with visual display units and handling of heavy load involving risk of back injury*. Those measures are of the greatest importance. However, due to a rather progressive approach Belgium has taken over the years regarding health and safety in this field, there has been no real impact of the EEC measures on Belgian legislation.

The Social Charter

Belgium has been among the champions in promoting the idea of a solemn EEC declaration of fundamental social rights, which was accepted by 11 of the Member States in Strasbourg, in December 1989 and in Maastricht in December 1991. The original idea came from Minister Hansenne, who, in 1986 on the occasion of the Belgian presidency, proposed to link the idea of flexibility to a 'socle' of unalienable social rights. However, Belgium is still one of the countries which has no social rights written in its Constitution and it seems that proposals to that end will not succeed; at the same time Belgium is one of the few remaining countries which has not yet ratified the European Social Charter, adopted in 1961 by the Council of Europe. That Charter has been adopted by both the Walloon and Flemish Parliaments.

Conclusion

The impact of European legislation on Belgian labour law and industrial relations has not been important, although influence in respect of freedom of movement, recognition of diplomas and the equal treatment of men and women was considerable.

Notes

1 R. Blanpain (1991) *International Encyclopaedia for Labour Law and Industrial relations*, Belgium, no. 164, Deventer, Kluwer.
2 B. Hepple (1990) *Comparative Labour Law and Industrial Relations*, R. Blanpain (ed.) 4th edn. Deventer, Kluwer, Chapter 12, *European Communities*, no. 41 *See also*: G. Schnorr and J. Egger (1990) 'European Communities', in *International Encyclopaedia for Labour Law and Industrial relations*, R. Blanpain, (ed.).

Chapter 17

Consumer protection

H. De Coninck

It is perhaps due to the favourable geographic position of Belgium and its open-market policy within Europe, that Belgian consumers have not had to wait for the Cecchini Report to ascertain how much they could benefit from a European market, at least as far as the prices of certain goods and services were concerned. This can be illustrated with the following three examples based on comparative price research by the Bureau Européen des Unions de Consommateurs (BEUC) and the Belgian consumer association Test Achats.

As far as products are concerned, a survey on car prices shows that the average price levels 'inclusive of taxes' and even 'net of taxes' in Belgium (and Luxemburg) remained very competitive (see Table 17.1). Compared to 1987, the price gap (up to 128 per cent) for inclusive prices has widened again, which is – paradoxically – alarming, taking into account the efforts by the Commission to limit the net price differences at 12 per cent (*cf.* Regulation 123/85, Commission notice no. 85/C17/03, and the formal complaint of BEUC to the Commission on 30 January 1990).

As for services, a study of package holidays in Mediterranean countries, offered by 107 catalogues of tour operators from eight European countries showed that for about two-thirds of the sample, price differences are over 40 per cent, reaching 90 per cent for some holidays, despite the relatively small differences between the relevant legal systems in these countries. So Belgian tourists enjoy a rather good protection combined with a relatively low price level.

In the field of financial services, there are similar differences. The most spectacular example concerns term insurance premiums, which are two-thirds less expensive in the UK than in Belgium. But, unlike active consumers of current consumer goods or services like package holidays, consumers of financial services meet a lot of obstacles on their way to buying foreign financial services, as we will explain below.

Table 17.1 *Relative average car price levels in 1986, 1987 and 1989 (cheapest price level = 100)*

Average price levels net of taxes												
1989	100	107	123	127	130	132	137	140	148	149	161	145
	DK	GR	B	L	NL	F	D	P	I	E	GB	IRL
1987	100.0	–	121.0	122.2	121.6	127.9	127.9	127.0	129.2	142.4	143.5	130.3
1986	100	–	121	122	123	130	129	136	144	146	151	151
Average price levels inclusive of all taxes												
1989	100	108	110	119	124	135	140	141	151	176	209	228
	L	B	D	F	I	NL	GB	E	P	IRL	DK	GR
1987	100.0	109.2	105.4	123.6	111.9	134.5	128.9	138.7	147.1	165.1	207.5	–
1986	100	110	107	125	122	136	138	142	164	185	210	–

Source: EEC study on car prices and progress towards 1992: *BEUC*, 15 October 1989, 37.

Consumer objectives

Free competition. Taking into account that consumer interests are best promoted by a transparent market with free competition (freedom of access and free delivery), the Community has to tackle a lot of present and potential restrictions of free competition such as (private or public) monopolies or oligopolies, price agreements, dumping, cartels, segmentation of the market(s), concentration and all forms of corporatism or protectionism (cf. Chapter 2). Some examples follow.

The EC Council started at last in 1988 with a first step of deregulation of the air traffic to open national markets, introducing three block exemption regulations in order to stimulate cooperation between national carriers. In the LEA (London European Airways) - Sabena case the Commission imposed a fine of 100,000 ECU on the latter, who had refused the access of the former to a computer-reservation system. Though the Commission could subject an important fusion between British Airways and British Caledonian in 1988 to severe conditions, Air France placed the Commission in January 1989 before an accomplished fact buying an important French competitor UTA, and hence controlling Air Inter and particularly Aéromaritime, which is a charter air carrier (competitor of Air France's Air Charter International); Aéromaritime had indeed offered very competitive air-tickets to consumers before. Everything points to the fact that Air France anticipated the EC Regulation on the control of concentrations which entered into force only on 21 September 1990.

Minimum harmonisation. Even when it would be possible to create effective competition within the Community, additional measures would be necessary to protect the consumer. Competition itself is not able to guarantee the protection of health, environment and even safety as far as these requirements remain voluntary and involve high costs. So far, the Commission has presented more than 200 directives to the Council, of which not half of them have been adopted. Only six directives contain substantial consumer protection measures (on misleading advertising, doorstep selling, consumer credit, product liability, toy safety, and package holidays), which have recently been introduced in Belgian law, notwithstanding the fact that the due dates were over several years ago. The Single Act (SA) does not include the protection of the consumer as an objective of the Treaty. The SA deems it sufficient that the Commission takes as a basis of the proposals 'a high level of consumer protection'.

Comparing on the one hand several optimistic Consumer Programmes with these scarce consumer protection directives on the other, we can only conclude — with BEUC — that so far the European consumer protection policy has failed. Different important projects or proposals did not reach a final stage until now: for example, contractual clauses and unfair contract terms, minimal warranties and after-sales service, trade practices, product safety and the setting up of an official 'Interpol' and recall system, access to justice and collective actions. Other proposals were (or are) in such a way amended by the Council that the results are doubtful for the consumers, at least for those in the most advanced countries, for example electronic fund transfer, money transfer in the EC, direct insurance other than life insurance, life insurance, car insurance, transborder television services, public transport, foodstuffs.

As far as Belgium is concerned, a systematic delay exists in applying the protection directives. After several warnings by the Commission, the Belgian government was brought into court. The government was condemned by the Court in two car-tax cases (10 April 1984 and 4 February 1988).

Though a majority of the realized EC directives and regulations concern technical requirements of all kinds of products, there is a fundamental lack of quality standards as a complement to basic health and safety requirements. Hence, the Commission should consider the creation of an independent body dealing with certification, labelling, and control of products and services. In 1990 the Commissioner for Consumer Affairs stated that the establishment of a European 'Food and Drug Administration' could be considered. Moreover, there is a lack of label conformity of foodstuffs, particularly as to nutritive value, which is partly due to many exemptions in the food sector. The introduction has been suggested, at least for basic foodstuffs, of European standards as to their definition, description and composition; the introduction of CE marks or CE labels based on quality, safety and durability criteria, could be considered.

Finally, as far as voluntary codes are concerned, we believe with the European Consumer Law Group (ECLG; *Journal of Consumer Policy*; 1983, 209) that such codes cannot be considered as a valuable alternative for legislation: in the best case they can be anticipatory, temporary and complementary to existing legislation. The latter provides technical, economic and protective measures, the former rather refers to social, cultural and other non-economic aspects of consumer matters. These last three aspects are very important in the (public) services area (*cf.* Reifner, 1989, 188).

In order to achieve consumer objectives, and to keep the balance between economic progress ('policy of supply') and consumer protection ('policy of demand'), national and European consumer organizations should cooperate better and the Commission should offer more financial resources and organize more effective consultation procedures, encouraging especially European-minded organizations without national or regional reflexes (*cf.* Reifner, p. 207).

EC legislation

In contradiction to the Community institutions' intentions, expressed in the successive Consumer Programmes, there is no Community consumer protection framework, which should be brought together in a European consumer code comprising all regulations about general health and safety, pricing, labelling, advertising, contractual clauses, post selling, door step selling, product and service liability, after-sales service and warranty, and effective individual and collective redress procedures.

There is no doubt that the failure of the Community in protecting the consumer within the Internal Market does not remain without consequences on a national level: first, national consumer protection legislation could be neglected in the same manner; second, the countries that stay behind in the field of consumer protection will not be stimulated to do better; and third, new national legislation could be limited to copy slavishly 'minimal' European directives and to drop more protective rules.

In trying to establish the freedom of services, the Community basically has three different options at hand which have different impacts on achieving the conflicting objectives: Internal Market and high level of consumer protection; first the Community may continue to recognize the unfettered applicability of the law of the receiving country as far as the marketing of services is concerned; this will maintain or lead to consumer protection discrimination between some Member States and to different rules for consumers and business, as has already happened in the insurance market (principle of 'nationalization' of consumer protective standards); a later effect could be a tendency of levelling down by the most 'consumer-minded' Member States, in order to remain competitive with 'industry-minded' Member States,; second: 'the Community may, as it has done in the past, harmonize by imposing certain protective standards in directives and allow free circulation there after' (principle of 'positive integration', which can be total or minimal); third, 'the Community may simply impose the standards of the country of origin to be valid in all countries where the services are marketed (principle of equivalence)'. This principle has been proposed in the White Paper on 'Completing the Internal Market' and is part of the 'New Approach'. Contrary to the first option where the 'host-country control' by the receiving country will be important for the consumer with regard to trade practices, the third option implies only a 'home-country control' by the exporting country: if certain conditions are fulfilled (e.g. conditions on establishment), service firms will be allowed to sell freely within the Internal Market. It is clear that the Community has chosen this liberal approach of 'mutual recognition', because it was impossible to realize a substantial positive integration or a minimal harmonization (second option) within a short time period (i.e. before 1993). This approach is at the same time pragmatic, on the one hand because the needed preparation of protective directives was and risks to remain considerable (it took c. 10 years to prepare the directives on misleading advertising and product liability), on the other hand because it seems easier to tackle consumer problems 'a posteriori' than to produce 'a priori' directives. Before going into more detail we stress that this 'New Approach' can cause or intensify tendencies of deregulation in some Member States, and the separation of markets of services and goods (e.g. in the car sector).

In the insurance market, and especially with regard to the directive of 22 June 1988 (non-life insurance) which makes a basic distinction between big commercial risks and mass risks (i.e. consumer risks), the 'New Approach' will eventually lead to perverse effects. Gains in comfortably protected and segregated consumer insurance markets, characterized by non-competitive premium rates, will subsidize losses in the highly competitive market for commercial risks'. Indeed, as far as mass risks are concerned, the Commission stated, taking into account several important Court decisions, but without consultation of consumer organizations, that – in the interest of the consumers (?) – free competition of non-life insurance services will be limited to big professional clients, who are presumed to be better informed and protected. In this way the 'infant' consumer will continue to 'enjoy' his normal nationally 'protected' insurance service, offered mainly by agreed companies. According to the Commission, this situation would only be provisional. These facts, combined with the growing concentration in the common insurance market puts the consumer in a not very enviable position.

It is hence unlikely that (non-life) insurance premiums in Belgium will diminish by 6 to 16 per cent as predicted in the Cecchini Report. It is indeed unlikely that the introduction of EC rules in Belgian law will considerably change the actual situation; it could on the contrary even lead to a decline of free competition or free entry. Moreover the Belgian Insurance Control Law of 9 July 1975 gives a broad interpretation to the notion of insurance contracts 'really concluded in Belgium' or 'considered as such, even if they are dated abroad': this broad definition increases our anxiety since contracts, concluded in Belgium with non-authorized or not exempted insurance companies, are legally void (see Claassens, H. and Cousy, H., 1989).

On 8 November 1990 the Commission enacted a directive on life insurance, which sets a first step into liberalization: in contradiction to the above mentioned non-life directive, this first life-insurance directive concerns individual life insurance which can be considered as a 'mass risk'. The main trump of taking a life insurance in Belgium and other countries consists in the fiscal allowance of the premiums under certain conditions. The loss of this fiscal advantage – it happens if a consumer signs an insurance with a foreign company – reduces the free choice of a cheaper foreign life insurance (in the UK) to a theoretical choice.

Such a fiscal discrimination is unacceptable and seems to be contrary to the EC Treaty. That is why the Belgian consumer association Test

Achats addressed in November 1989 a complaint to the Commission against the Belgian State (see Test Achats/Budget & Droits, 1990, 2). Finally, it should be noted that contracts, concluded at the initiative of a foreign life-insurance firm, are submitted to the control rules of the host country, or the so-called 'risk-country control', namely the control by the Member State where the consumer lives.

The existing banking directives of 24 June 1988 on the liberalization of capital movements and of 15 December 1989 on banking solvency and minimum capital requirements pursue an Internal Market for banking services. According to the first banking directive every EC citizen is free (since 1 July 1990) to open a bank account, to deposit his savings on a deposit book, to invest his savings, to lend money and to hold foreign currencies in any bank within the Internal Market. At first sight and from an economic point of view this directive will not change that much for Belgian citizens, whereas many savers discovered a long time ago the benefits of interest competition on savings and investment. The same can be said about common investment funds, which were already regulated since the UCITS directive of 20 December 1985. From a consumer point of view, the main problems and dangers in the opening financial-service market seem to be: the lack of adequate information, the lack of protection of the consumer and particularly of the little share holder (*cf.* Counye R., 1989, 5).

Fortunately, these financial directives do not introduce a discrimination between big transactions and mass transactions as happened in the insurance sector, but on the other hand they offer the same disadvantages of the 'New Approach': all 'marketing rules', i.e. rules on information, description of the offer, advertising, prospectus may be enacted by the country of origin; further, the home-country control applies; and finally the receiving host country may only exceptionally enforce its legal provisions when they 'are justified on the grounds of the public good' (Article 19 paragraph 3 of the SA). For the same reasons as developed above, the Commission should at least set minimum standards.

There is not only a lack of information with regard to the supply of banking services, but also as far as little share holders are concerned. Once again Belgium had to wait for a European incentive (in 1985) before enacting national legislation about the information which must be published when a firm or financial group takes or obtains an important part of a society, which is quoted on the stock exchange. According to the directive of 12 December 1988, a new law of 2 March 1989 was voted. Taking into account the French takeover of the Belgian Société Générale, the scope of the law has been widened: it deals not only with transparency rules, but also with measures on public takeover bids (OPA).

We cannot pass by one of the most important current 'revolutions': transborder television services linked to telecommunications and our ever-breeding computer society. Though a new wind is blowing through and around traditional public institutions with regards to TV and telecommunications, improving efficiency and competition, we should consider and tackle in good time the emerging side-effects and abuses. If it is true that the TEC directive of 3 October 1989 on the coordination of the different national legislations in the TV area improves competition and introduces a minimal protection as to advertising and especially as far as young consumers are concerned (with regards to pornography and violence), the directive has been introduced rather late (national implementation before 3 October 1991), and seems to underestimate the diminution of 'Spectrum tightness' since cable TV and new technologies have been broadened. Hence, the economic base of regulation has been undermined. Moreover the new technologies, like teleselling, teletext and viewdata, increase direct relations on the television services market. As far as Belgium is concerned, the (quasi) advertising monopoly of the private VTM-commercial television – in contrast to the public national stations (BRT) – seems to be inconsistent with free competition principles, and can bring about economic inefficiencies and even abuses of economic power position.

Conclusions

Since the Community policy has been a failure, its influence on Belgian policy has been minimal. As consumer protection arguments are sometimes abused both by national professional organizations or by national or Community authorities to maintain existing situations or to prevent harmonization, consumer organizations should adopt a pragmatic approach on the completion of the Internal Market: on the one hand they plead for an unconditional opening of the national markets and a free competition in a transparent common market, on the other hand they plead for adequate and fast measures from the Community institutions when abuses or shortcomings are established (either regulations, directives or Community actions). Complementary to these future legal 'a posteriori' interventions, consumer organizations consider certain forms of consumer dialogue or the enactment of codes, model contracts or arbitration schemes as a useful and temporary complement of legal instruments, but in no way as an alternative.

References

Claasens, H. and Cousy, H. (1989), 'Het juridisch kader van de interne verzekeringsmacht', *Tijdschrift voor Belgisch Handelrecht*.

Counye, R. (1989), 'Investisseur dans l'Europe 1992', *Marché Commun et Services Financiers*, 30/31 January, BEUC/AgV.

'Non-legislative means of consumer protection' (1983), *Journal of Consumer Policy*, no. 6.

Reifner, U. (1989), 'Marché Commun de services financiers', *Cahiers de la Consommation*.

Test Achats - Budget & Droits (1990) February.

Chapter 18

National identity and cultural policy

M.A.G. van Meerhaeghe

It will be clear from Chapter 1 that education and culture are fields which fall within the competence of the member countries. There is no reference to them in the Rome Treaty nor in the Single Act. Nevertheless, some propose an addition to the EC Treaty, entrusting the care of cultural life exclusively to the various cultural communities, in order to prevent 'the meddlesome Brussels bureaucracy' from intervening in cultural life (Mourik 1991: 82).

Since the model table of contents (*cf.* Table A in the series introduction) mentions 'European identity and cultural policies', it may be useful to consider the concept of European identity and the corresponding national notion. Indeed, many member countries want to 'maintain' their 'cultural identity' or avoid 'the loss of national identity'.

Definitions

Culture and civilization contribute to determining the (national or European) identity (e.g. what is Belgium?), which involves for the people concerned common interests, a common history and a common destiny. Since there are hundreds of definitions of civilization and culture (Kroeber and Kluckhohn 1952), a definition to begin with may be appropriate. Civilization is the state of being civilized (endowed with law and order and a standard of living favouring arts and sciences). Culture relates to the artistic and scientific aspects of civilization (although many define it as social environment).

From a macroeconomic point of view culture bears on the acquired knowledge (notably the standards) of a specific community. The results of intellectual and artistic activity which have emerged in the course of the centuries constitute the culture of the various peoples. Reciprocal influence is finding increasing expression. (Chopin and da Vinci do not have their impact only on their national culture.) Even after the disappearance of certain communities the influence of their culture persists. Hence it is that Roman culture lives on (Meerhaeghe 1986: 153).

EC and European identity

As mentioned above, the Treaty does not refer to education and culture; nevertheless the Community is trying to 'harmonize'. This meets strong opposition, for example, from the German *Länder* and the Belgian (cultural) Communities, responsible for these fields. They reproach the German and Belgian (federal) governments with usurping their powers in their dealings with the European Community. One wonders why the harmonization of vocational training is necessary for the establishment of economic union.

The Commission approved several educational programmes since 1977, but 'even if reiterated for years, they seemed to have a rather rhetorical character' (Mohr 1990, 234). Moreover, some programmes – such as Erasmus – were more related to economic objectives (competitiveness of the Community). A similar observation applies to the cultural programmes. The priorities seem to be: promotion of the audiovisual sector and books, training for cultural purposes, and cooperation to strengthen 'the consciousness of a common cultural heritage as part of a European identity'.

European identity 'is what time was for Saint Augustine – obvious until you ask what it is; ephemeral when you try to define it; undeniable as an intuitive experience, beyond our grasp as an object of thought' (Savario Vertone quoted by Ripa 1987: 10). The definition of European identity, approved by the European ministers of Foreign Affairs and published in Copenhagen on 14 December 1973, refers to the diversity of cultures within the framework of a common European civilization, the attachment to common values and principles, the increasing convergence of attitudes to life, common specific interests and the willingness to participate in the European construction. This definition is too vague and does not stress what is typical for Europe and what distinguishes it from the US. Some deny the existence of a European culture (they admit the existence of a European cultural area) and of a European civilization (Domenach 1990: 80–81).

While in the US all groups of immigrants were and are forced to 'melt' within the US political system and to adopt its language (cf. the reaction to the use of Spanish), Europe consists of several separate but homogeneous cultural entities. The US is a multiracial society; so far Europe is not, although influential international forces favour such multiracialism and foster the corresponding population flows. Moreover, immigration from Islamic countries contributes to the expansion of non-European elements (in some cities there are more mosques than churches).

A common history has accustomed European countries to take into account their neighbours' policies. There is a willingness to discuss common problems and a feeling of belonging to the same continent, thanks to centuries of cross-fertilization. As Hugh Seton-Watson (1985: 9) puts it: 'The growth of an increasingly homogeneous European culture, and also a belief among thinking men and women that they belong to a single, even if diverse, European cultural community, are facts of history and facts of this present time. The notion of a European cultural community, allegiance to which transcended, but did not normally contradict allegiance to a more precise regional or national sovereignty, is derived, I think, from an earlier allegiance to Christendom, and this in turn has its antecedents.'

The relative importance of the different national cultures has changed in the course of the centuries. Italian culture dominated in the sixteenth and seventeenth centuries, French culture in the eighteenth century. Dominant economies may be dominant civilizations, they are not necessarily dominant cultures (the US). Post-war Italian culture was and is relatively more significant than the economy to which it corresponds. European diversity risks disappearance through the progressive internationalization emanating chiefly from the US, its uniformity of products, advertising and ways of life. European television is invaded by American series. Europe must insist on its 'Europeanness'. If we may paraphrase Massimo d'Azeglio: 'We have made Europe, now we must make Europeans.'

Differences between the US and Europe

It is an heroic simplification to talk about 'American' and 'European' identities or cultures, given, for example, the many 'subcultures' in Europe. Some authors, such as the American sociologist P. Sorokin, see no difference between American and European cultures. They talk about 'Atlantic' or 'Western' cultures. European immigration brought to the US European values on which American culture is based. But two centuries of separate development have created important differences. Moreover, in the US the Anglo-Saxon element has weakened to a large extent. There is no unanimity of values characterizing respectively American and European culture. The proposed criteria are vague and not always convincing. Values characteristic for Europe would be ability of synthesis, concern for equilibrium, which would imply the rejection of — even legitimate — values threatening to become exclusive or hypertrophic (Piovene 1955: 424–25). André Maurois (1955: 186) praises 'our sense of moderation, our need of nuances, our taste'.

Materialism and adoration of technological progress would be typical for the United States. A lack of culture is related to this materialism. It is a classical reproach. As Georges Clemenceau put it: 'America? That is the development from barbarity to decadence without the detour through culture.' (Wagner 1977: 23). Is the US a melting pot? It is a persistently segmented (not fragmented) society (Kammen 1972), each part having its own lifestyle.

The social tensions would be higher than in Europe. Robot pictures of the American and the European came into being. The American is less civilized and immediately calls everybody by his first name, but his friendliness is artificial ('this friendliness does not necessarily mean that the Americans are interested in long-lasting, intimate friendships': *The Economist* 1989: 40). The European is more formal and distant. The former is impulsive and simplistic, the latter cautious and thoughtful. More than the American, the European is proud of his or her history. Hence his or her tendency to know best. When he or she has to take into account both aesthetic and practical considerations, the European tends to be influenced by the first, the American by the second. What distinguishes Europe from the United States, according to Paul Henri Spaak, is its greater individualism. He explains the difference by an anecdote: 'When a European woman enters a room and sees another woman wearing the same dress she is furious. If an American woman does not see at least five other women wearing the same dress she is afraid she is badly dressed.' Nevertheless Spaak exaggerates. The earliest visitors to the United States, such as Tocqueville and Lord Brice, were already struck by the individualism, the self-confidence and the sense of initiative of the Americans. More than the European, the American is sensitive to praise and criticism. This does not date from the present time. Tocqueville already found this: Americans insist on being praised, and if you do not do it, they praise themselves. Europe has long been the centre of science. Paul Valéry (1957: 995–6) stresses its scientific vocation. 'Europe . . . this little cape of the Asian continent . . . falls victim to a perpetual unrest and research.' 'Europe . . . reaches the top . . . of intellectual fertility, richness and ambition.' Europe is 'der Geist der stets verneint' (Goethe 1923: 67). But if Europe was strong in invention, it was not in its application. Europe invented the body-scanner, the US developed it, but Japan sells it. In 1941 the German Conrad Zuse invented the programmable computer, but after the war the British Army did not even examine it. In 1951 Ferranti (Manchester) produced the first electronic computer, but IBM commercialized it two years later. Another small British firm created the video-recorder in 1961, but did not start its production.

Belgian identity

Given the absence of a Community cultural policy, it is quite to be expected that its influence on Belgian cultural policy has been minimal. In 1991–92 Belgium received 1,963,700 Ecu for the Erasmus

Programme (1.2 million Ecu in 1990–91, 0.8 million in 1989–90, 0.4 million in 1988–89), but even if Belgium withdrew from the Community, it would be no problem to provide a similar small amount to Belgian students (especially since Belgium is a net contributor to the Community).

Belgium has been called a non-country (Claes 1985: 198), an historical accident and a result of rivalry between European 'powers'. Given the two main linguistic communities in Belgium, Dutch-speaking Flemings (5,484,000) and French-speaking Walloons (2,868,000; there are also 57,000 German-speaking Belgians; *cf.* chapter 16), 'uncertain(ty) of its own identity' (*The Economist* 1990: 24) is not surprising. Instead of a Belgian identity, Flemish and Walloon identities exist. The existence of Belgians is even denied. As the Belgian politician Jules Destrée told King Albert: 'Sire, il n'y a pas de Belges'.

Nevertheless, there is some affinity between the Flemings and the Walloons. Linguistic links between the Flemings and the Dutch on the one hand, and the Walloons and the French on the other hand favour cultural relations; they do not imply a desire for political unity nor do they detract from separate Flemish and Walloon identities. Brussels, originally a Flemish town, was largely frenchified. Its population (706,000) is perhaps the most 'Belgian' part of Belgium. The foreigners, who tend to adopt the French language, number 238,000 in Flanders, 367,000 in Wallonia and 264,000 in Brussels (1 January 1989). The Flemings consider the Belgian state as an instrument of former oppression and are indifferent to that state. The Walloons resent their inferior economic position and show a similar, though smaller, apathy towards the state; they are more 'Belgian'.

Flemings as well as Walloons are above all tied to their villages and towns. Hence their political indifference, which is greatest in Flanders. As in the rest of Europe but to a larger extent, their town and country planning is horrible, as Brussels illustrates. They are Breughelian, individualists, shrewd, opposed to state intervention, although the Walloons less than the Flemings (Coudenberg). To some extent some inhabitants of Flanders, Brussels and Wallonia feel more European than Belgian. This may be a result of a progressing Community and a disintegrating Belgium.

The EC and the Belgian cultural communities

Economic power may lead to hegemony in the communication sector, as the example of the US and its worldwide media network proves. It can have important cultural repercussions. Turning out, for example, competitive software programmes of quality implies huge investments and a coordinated effort of all European nations. It is urgent that they 'begin now to plan a European television news programme to be reproduced by a pool of private interests. If we do not the Americans will soon monopolize our screens with news programmes of their own for Europe' (Ripa de Meana 1987: 14.)

Although the cultural communities in Europe are equal, some are more equal than others. Small communities' cultural contributions (e.g. in the field of film production) are often as important as those of large communities, but they are handicapped by the absence of economies of scale. Because of their limited markets, small linguistic and cultural communities, such as the Flemish community, face higher costs. And the conquest of the larger markets implies expensive translations. '*Dallas* is not on practically all European TV screens because it is better than European productions, but because after amortization on the domestic market it can be offered to the whole world at dumping-level prices.' There is also 'a lot of condescension *vis-à-vis* smaller entities' (Mourik 1991: 81), as can be seen in the European bureaucracy.

Some Community decisions are harmful to the cultural positions of smaller countries, such as Belgium, and are partly due to the linguistic imperialism of some Member States. The Commission is, for example, opposed to fixed book prices and to cultural subsidies, both essential for small cultural entities.

Brussels as seat of the Commission

The presence of many civil servants of the Community is resented by a lot of inhabitants of the Brussels region and Flemish Brabant. The additional demand of about 20,000 Eurocrats raises prices of soil and rents. Since the European civil servants do not make any effort to be integrated in the local communities and seem not to have any intention of becoming so, relations between the local population and the much richer immigrants leave much to be desired. Eurocrats have their own schools and associations and live too much in a ghetto (*Le Monde* 1992). Professor Van Impe (Brussels University) even refers to 'the colonization of Brussels and Flemish Brabant by well-to-do foreign barbarians' (Tastenhoye 1992). Many Flemings (and Flemish cultural associations) would like the seat of the Community institutions to be transferred to another Member State. But the building industry's lobbies are influential.

'Colonization' is especially the case on Flemish territory. When they learn another language, international civil servants tend to learn French; very few learn the less 'international' Dutch. Thus the presence of the Eurocrats becomes a frenchifying factor. In 1992 a Flemish Christian parlimentarian even proposed a resolution in the Flemish council in respect of protection of the Dutch language 'endangered by the evolution on the European level'; approval of the treaty of Maastricht should be withheld if protection of the Dutch language is not guaranteed (Suykerbuyk). In fact, the European Communities use only French and English as working languages (notwithstanding German protest.)

The cultural danger of European integration on Belgium consists not only in frenchifying but also in anglicising. English is more and more used in higher education and research. In the Community larger countries have little respect for the languages of smaller countries. This applies to the Court of Justice as well. The Commercial Court of Leuven (Belgium) submitted a question for a preliminary ruling on the interpretation of Article 30 of the EEC Treaty and Article 14 of Directive 79/112/EEC (labelling and presentation of foodstuffs for sale to the consumer; labelling in the language of the place where the product is offered for sale). BVBA Peeters markets French and German mineral waters in the Flemish-speaking region of Belgium. The plaintiffs considered that Peeters was operating in breach of Belgian legislation since the bottles were labelled only in French or German, whereas in the Flemish region the labels should be in Dutch. The Court held that the above-mentioned Article and Directive 'preclude national legislation which requires exclusively the use of a given language for the labelling of foodstuffs without allowing for the use of another language easily understood by consumers or for consumer legislation to be provided by other measures' (Case C-369/89 of 18 June 1991). So the man in the street in Flanders will have to learn other languages in order to know more about the foodstuffs offered for sale! Even the European Court seems in favour of linguistic imperialism.

Conclusion

Although the European treaties do not provide for a European cultural policy, the Commission approved several action programmes in this field. Since their implementation was very limited, it is small wonder that their impact on the Member States' policies was unimportant. Like other small countries, Belgium fears that a cultural integration could turn into a loss of national identity. 'Europeanness' will be furthered by the defence of national identities, not by 'harmonization'. Cultural dominance is resented all the more in a country involved in French economic imperialism (*cf.* Chapter 3).

The repercussions of the presence in Brussels of a large number of rich Eurocrats are not without disadvantages. Many Belgians would like the seat of the Commission and other Community institutions to be transferred elsewhere. They do not consider this seat as a benefit for Belgium, as the Commission seems to do.

References

Claes, Lode (1985), *De afwezige meerderheid*, Leuven, Davidsfonds.

Coudenberg (Groep) (1987), *Rapport Coudenberg. Naar een ander België?*, Tielt, Lannoo.

Domenach, Jean-Marie (1990), *Europe: le défi culturel*, Paris, La Découverte.

Goethes Faust. Der Tragödie erster Teil (1923), Leipzig, Meulenhoff.

Kammen, Michael (1972), *People of paradox. An enquiry concerning the origins of American civilization*, New York.

Kroeber, A.L. and Kluckhohn, C. (s.d. — published 1952), *Culture. A critical review of concepts and definitions*, New York, Knopf, Random House.

Maurois, A. (1955) 'L'esprit américain', *Le Nouveau Monde et l'Europe*, Brussels, Office de Publicité.

Meerhaeghe, M.A.G. van (1986), 'Culture and economics', *Economia delle Scelte Pubbliche*, Anno IV, No. 3, September—December.

Mohr Brigitte (1990), 'Education and culture', in *Federal Republic of Germany and EC membership evaluated*, ed. C.C. Schweitzer and D. Karsten, London, Pinter.

Mourik, Maarten (1991) 'Cultural coexistence: Europe needs a European cultural charter to protect the cultural integrity of smaller communities and preserve Europe's cultural variety', *European Affairs*, April—May, Vol. 5, No. 2.

Piovene, G. (1955) 'Conférence de M. Guido Piovene' in *Le Nouveau Monde et l'Europe*, Brussels, Office de Publicité.

Ripa di Meana, Carlo (1987) 'The intercultural society we call Europe', *European Affairs*, autumn No. 3.

Seton-Watson, Hugh (1985) 'What is Europe, where is Europe? From mystique to politique', *Encounter, July–August*.

'Students: Not at home' (1989) *The Economist*, 19 July.

Suykerbuyk, Herman (1992) *Voorstel van resolutie van de heer H. Suykerbuyk c.s. betreffende de bescherming van de Nederlandse taal*, Vlaamse Raad, s.d.

Tastenhoye, Guido (1992) 'Van Impe: Koloniale eurocratie in Brusselse is intocht der barbaren' *Gazet van Antwerpen*, 18 February.

Valéry, Paul (1957) *Oeuvres*, Paris, Gallimard, La Pléiade.

Wagner, Wolfgang (1977) 'The Europeans' image of America' in *America and Western Europe*, ed. Karl Kaiser and Hans-Peter Schwarz, Lexington Mass., Lexington Books.

'Who wants what in the brave new Europe?' (1990) *The Economist*, 1 December.

CONCLUSION

Chapter 19

Summary and conclusion

M.A.G. van Meerhaeghe

Hereafter a summary of the main findings of the preceding chapters is provided. Where appropriate it is supplemented by additional comments by the editor. Finally a few conclusions follow.

Summary

Economic policy

Since Community action must be seen in connection with its objectives, chapter 1 examines these goals. The competition principle has a predominant influence on the Treaty. Adherence to the subsidiarity principle is considered to be an essential element in an appropriate balance of power within the Community.

According to the subsidiarity principle, several aspects of economic policy should be better left to member countries. This is the case, for example, with regional policies. They have not been successful either in the Community or in Belgium. The same is true of industrial policies, which, moreover, do not respect the strong anti-interventionist philosophy of the Treaty. This is the reason why they are not extensively discussed in separate chapters, but examined in this introductory chapter.

Chapter 2 considers the differences between a recent Belgian law and Community competition rules. Since Community legislation is directly applicable in the Member States, national legislation in this field (especially in small countries such as Belgium) is not justified.

Given the direct application, we would expect governments to keep an eye on the preparation of Community competition legislation. This seems not to be the case because the Community competition policy is far from satisfactory. It is characterized by incoherence, dogmatism, obscurity and, hence, insecurity for the companies concerned. It sometimes takes into account considerations which have nothing to do with competition policy.

It is argued in chapter 3 on internal market policy that the evolution of Belgium's economy without the EC would not have been very different from the actual expansion. After all, third countries, such as Norway, Sweden, Switzerland and Austria, realize growth rates superior to that of Belgium. Indeed the EC effect is impossible to measure.

Among the characteristics of Belgium's economic structure are openness and internationalization, the dominance of medium-sized enterprises, many rigidities (especially in the social sector) and specialization in products for which international demand is rather weak. A handicap is the fact that main decision-centres are situated abroad (foreign firms having acquired Belgian banks and other companies).

We could say that before European integration agricultural policy was to a large extent social policy with economic features. After it, it was rather economic policy accompanied by social measures (chapter 4). The common agricultural policy meant the exposure of Belgian agriculture to more efficient agricultural systems. Belgian decision-makers (government and farm organizations) adopted a policy which transformed Belgian agriculture.

Existing regional differences were strengthened by divergent responses to the common agricultural policy. The Walloon farms concentrated their activities more on traditional crops for which price support was strongest (cereals and milk). Flemish farms privileged 'modern' crops offering better possibilities abroad (pig breeding, horticulture). Environmental problems relative to agriculture alarm public opinion. The increased use of fertilizers, for example, has affected the quality of surface and underground water.

Farms are more and more specialized and investment is directed towards equipment and buildings for one specific crop or activity. Increased concentration and productivity could not prevent family income – the Belgian farm is a family farm – lagging behind non-farm income. Belgium's share in the Community agriculture is also declining. It is difficult to measure the EC impact on Belgian agriculture. A hypothetical evolution without a common agricultural policy would probably have been different from an extrapolation of the pre-EC development; to what extent is only a matter of guesswork.

EC transport policy has been the victim of conflicts between free-market advocates and champions of dirigism and protectionism. The Community did not succeed in achieving a common transport market. Structural problems in road transport (e.g. cabotage), inland waterways (overcapacity) and railways (lack of cooperation between national companies) could not be solved. Prices of European air services are substantially higher than would obtain in a competitive market. The influence on national markets has been limited, especially on the Belgian market. It explains the absence of a chapter on transport policy.

The lack of a European transport policy is especially detrimental to small countries. In order to benefit by economies of scale, they need larger markets; Belgium's openness does not guarantee reciprocity.

Only the Single Act mentions environmental policy and the Community policy is hesitant. This is strange, since in this field international cooperation is more necessary than elsewhere. Moreover, it is one of the few sectors where the market alone cannot solve problems. The Belgian policy leaves much to be desired (chapter 5). Little or no progress has been made in most sectors (water, waste, noise, soil). Some success was obtained in the field of air pollution, but 50 per cent of this was due to the reduction of industrial emissions in Germany. There are only a few European directives, but Belgium manages not to implement them. The European Court condemned Belgium, although non-implementation is due to regional authorities. The central government has no power to intervene at the regional level. Since Belgium's environmental policy is behind those of the neighbouring countries, the Community policy – although limited and prudent – is a stimulus for Belgium's policy.

Chapter 6 stresses that there is no universally accepted view on the relation between economic integration and taxes, government expenses or even budget deficits. The Treaty does not provide for budgetary integration. But a member, and especially a small member, of a group of countries striving for more cooperation, has to take into account the policies of the other members and to adjust to these policies. Small countries have a lower degree of freedom of setting objectives. This would be the case even if the EC did not exist.

The EC's impact on Belgium's budgetary policy has been limited. The VAT system had to be adopted and some types of subsidies eliminated. The increased capital mobility – a phenomenon more international than European – precluded the use of certain policy instruments (for example, an increased taxation of capital). Commission advice to Belgium in relation to the budget deficit had little influence, although it was helpful in convincing public opinion of the necessity of reducing the deficit. Although fiscal policy has only an indirect effect on the competitive position, a high budgetary deficit may give rise to problems on the foreign-exchange market and necessitate monetary-policy measures.

In order to maintain its competitive position and since the Deutschmark (DM) is the leading currency in Europe (and the anchor of the European Monetary System), Belgium has pursued a policy of stabilizing its DM exchange rate (chapter 7). Such a policy not only implies a monetary policy similar to that of Germany, but also similar supplementing policies (such as fiscal policy and wages policy). Since such supplementing policies were lacking in 1974–81, Belgium was obliged to devalue by 8.5 per cent in February 1982. The monetary policy pursued would have been necessary even without the membership of the EC. The dual exchange rate, abolished in 1990, provided only a limited freedom to policy-makers (as a cushion for speculative attacks).

Foreign relations

Chapter 8 – which introduces Part 2 devoted to international relations – illustrates the openness of the Belgian economy, which is much higher than in similar small economies. This openness implies a higher sensitivity to external factors. It is very difficult to estimate the EC effect on trade.

During the 1960s there was an important increase in trade with the EC, especially with Germany and France. Belgium's external trade is characterized by important intra-branch commerce, even more than in other member countries. Its exports contain a large amount of products for which world demand is low. Neither factors are due to an EC effect.

In the field of commercial policy the Community received extensive and exclusive powers from the member countries. The main advantage of the common commercial policy is the Community's larger bargaining power. However, it is impossible to prove whether it equals or differs from the disadvantages resulting from a common policy which does not necessarily look after Belgium's interest. Moreover, the common policy sometimes gives rise to retaliation by third countries, detrimental to Belgium.

Although neither the European Political Cooperation (EPC) nor the Western European Union (WEU) come within the Community framework, they may be considered as elements in the process of European construction (chapter 9). There is still no European foreign policy since EPC Member States retain almost complete control over their national diplomacy. It implies that the cost of EPC is small, while its benefits (exchange of information, higher diplomatic weight and mutual support, creation of an external image) are not unimportant. Maastricht may be a (hesitant) beginning.

The EC lacks a security dimension. The Member States are only 'ready to coordinate their positions more closely on the political and economic aspects of security' (Single Act). Nine Member States reactivated the WEU, although they retain sovereignty in defence matters. Belgium favours a communitarization of the Twelve's foreign and security policies. A communitarized policy will have a greater weight in world affairs, but will not necessarily take into account Belgium's position (a world directorate would still more ignore Belgium's interests). A communitarized policy in respect of less-developed countries would also present many advantages and avoid duplications (chapter 10). But the national contribution for EC 'development' policy represent only a fraction of credits for national 'development' policy. Moreover the Community policy has not been successful. The level of living in Africa is lower than during the colonial period. However, the main reasons are the shortcomings of the governments of the less-developed countries concerned.

Political and legal system

Since the war Belgium has always been present when European integration was being discussed (chapter 11). Indeed, good relations with its neighbours are essential to Belgium's survival. It cannot safeguard its independence or attain prosperity in isolation. Belgium played a key role in the negotiations leading to the European Community.

Belgium has always favoured a supranational Europe (giving more power to the Parliament) and – implicitly – majority voting. The supranational concept does not clash with feelings of regional identity. Indeed, within the Community a greater regional autonomy can be pursued without the risk of detrimental repercussions. The EC brought Belgium a solution to the Franco–German rivalry, which twice threatened its existence, and a means of greater participation in decisions formerly settled by greater powers.

Chapter 12 examines the Community's influence on democracy. Belgium's membership caused a constitutional amendment giving legitimacy to the transfer of sovereignty and devolution of powers to the Community. However, criticism is voiced about a transfer to institutions lacking democratic legitimacy. Intergovernmental conferences in various fields of law take decisions without any parliamentary control.

On the benefit side the Community paved the way for new rules in the Belgian legal order: the principle of equality between men and women and the protection of the environment. Although it is not a European Community institution, the influence of the European Court on Human Rights has been considerable. Elementary rules relating to the public character of hearings or to the right of defence have been forced upon through landmark decisions of the Court. On the whole, however, the Community influence has not been essential. This also applies to the principle of the Rule of Law, which developed in Belgium in parallel with its application in the Court of Justice.

The influence of Community law culminated in the decision of the Belgian Supreme Court of 27 May 1970 (chapter 13). It introduced the principle of the primacy of rules of international law and Community law in the Belgian legal system. Since 1970 Belgium has evolved from being a unitary and centralized state into a state comprised of four formally recognized language regions, three communities and three regions which are territorial entities (chapter 14). This complex, typically Belgian federal system was built independently of the European construction. It is also characterized by the absence of the primacy of federal law (in contradiction to the rule in a federal system). Neither have European federal ideas influenced the Belgian state reform. The Flemish and Walloon regions favour a Europe of regions and these policies could be felt in the future on a European level.

A major change introduced in the state reform could serve as a useful precedent at the EC level. It gives to any citizen a direct jurisdictional recourse to the Court of Arbitration for any violation of the principle of equality of the Belgians. The principle of federal loyalty – a principle of EC law (*cf.* e.g. Article 5 of the Rome Treaty) – has noticeably influenced Belgian public law, in particular in relation to the federalization process. For example, it implies the obligation for a sub-division of the state to perform correctly under the obligations set forth by law and not to make an abusive usage of its competences.

Social and cultural policies

On the basis of available official figures (1985) chapter 15 concludes that the EC has not led to a substantial labour inflow (although it admits that the inflow was high in some sectors). Three-quarters of the inflow was from other EC countries (a large part of it occurred before 1958) and from Spain and Portugal before 1986. It is argued that a direct transfer of labour was substituted by trade in goods.

In the field of labour law and industrial relations, the European impact has been rather marginal, as in other member countries (Chapter 16). Article 48 of the Rome Treaty guarantees free movement of labour, but Belgium had to be cited before the European Court as to the implementation of regulations based on that article. Belgium adapted its legislation to several directives (such as those on collective redundancies, on the safeguarding of employees' rights in the events of transfers of undertakings, businesses or part of businesses and on the protection of employees in the event of the insolvancy of their employer).

Belgium also took into account European legislation on the equal treatment of men and women as regards access to employment, vocational training and promotion, and working conditions. Here again a number of Belgian cases were brought before the European Court. Although Belgium is among the promotors of the idea of a solemn Community declaration on social rights, it is one of the few countries which have not ratified the European social charter (although the Walloon and Flemish parliaments have done so).

According to several surveys, prices in Belgium are competitive in many sectors (cars, package holidays). In other sectors much is to be done (e.g. air travel). Moreover, subsidies have distorted competition (chapter 17). So far, the Council has only approved a few important directives related to consumer protection. They have been introduced in Belgian law with great delay. Other Commission proposals were amended in such a way that they are only of minor significance to consumers in the most advanced countries (money transfer, life insurance, car insurance, package holidays). The Community failure of consumer protection has repercussions on the member countries: the countries staying behind, such as Belgium, are not stimulated to improve consumer protection.

Chapter 18 considers European and Belgian identities and cultural policies. European culture is characterized by diversity and the feeling of belonging to the same continent. Belgian identity refers either to Flemish or Walloon identities. Nevertheless, both population groups seem as close to each other as to foreign, same language-speaking populations. Some decisions of EC institutions were seen to be harmful to small cultural communities.

Conclusion

In the economic field the membership's repercussions on Belgium have been rather limited. A common foreign and security policy is still wishful thinking. The EC's policy in respect of less-developed countries has only has a marginal influence on Belgium's corresponding policy.

Belgium is a net contributor to the Community (approximately 50 billion francs). Against that, the benefits from hosting the EC institutions are sometimes mentioned. But the corresponding disadvantages are felt more and more, especially in respect of housing. Insufficient linguistic adaptation by Community civil servants is also deplored, mainly in the Flemish periphery. Transfer of the Brussels institutions to other countries is even suggested.

The EC was, in fact, established to bind and control Germany. As such it was beneficial to Belgium, invaded twice by that country, although Germany had good reason not to be enthusiastic about the Versailles Treaty. But a similar 'guarantee' could and has been provided through the membership of other organizations.

As for the repercussions in the political and legal system, Belgium's membership caused a constitutional amendment legitimating the transfer of sovereignty and devolution of power to the Community. Membership has given rise to new rules in the legal order, but there was no influence on the implementation of the Rule of Law.

On the whole the EC's influence has not been as important as many Community and Belgian official publications contend.

Dangers

A less favourable turn is even possible in several fields. In the monetary sector, for example, the European Monetary System (EMS) works as a DM bloc. The other member countries try to align their monetary policy with that of Germany. It was not Germany that decided that the DM should be the dominant currency. The markets did that.

One of the most important aims of Germany is to control inflation. Germany's successful anti-inflation policy forced the other member countries to match that success. Even non-EC countries, such as Switzerland

and Austria, link their currencies to the DM.

Germany's grip on the EC and its fairly independent monetary policy explain why the EMS works. It is not without disadvantages for Germany. The DM became one of the major international currencies. In the official holdings of foreign exchange the dollar accounts for 60 per cent, the DM for 21 per cent and the yen for 10 per cent.

In fact, the DM has become *the* European currency, a role initially devoted to the ECU. Some member countries, such as France and the United Kingdom, resent Germany's monetary dominance. Hence, the Maastricht proposals for a European monetary union, a central European bank and a European currency, the ECU.

A central European bank runs the risk of being a politicized institution. Only two central banks in the Community are to a certain degree independent of their governments. There is a danger that the Community could be sacrificing a stable, hard currency – the DM which is the anchor of the EMS – without knowing what it would be getting in return.

Present political trends are in favour of the transfer of as many fields of competence from the national state to smaller communities, not of the transfer from the national state to an international bureaucracy.

President de Gaulle was perhaps too severe when he called the Commission 'Quelque aéropage technocratique, apatride et irresponsable' (9 September 1965). But it must be admitted that the Commission's neglect of the subsidiarity principle and its tendency to 'harmonize' everything under the sun has been harmful to Member States.

'The Common Market experience' is still 'a baroque thing of complex and inconsistent themes and inversions' (Cleveland 1969: 87). Bureaucracy could not be avoided. The Community is characterized by 'regulations of Byzantine complexity and infinite number (and) ultra-bureaucratic procedures' (Johnson 1987: 15).

The more the subsidiarity principle is mentioned, the less it is applied. Maastricht, once again, would lead to more power for the Community. This centralization is especially harmful to the smaller countries.

Americanization threatens European identities and especially the cultures of smaller countries. The danger is manifold. Americanization could be the outcome should Europe not work out an independent foreign policy, but rather were to act as a US satellite.

The inevitability of the Gulf War was never proven. Following the invasion neither sanctions nor negotiations were given a chance. Many similar aggressions, even in the same region (Lebanon, Cyprus), have never been 'punished'. All over the world there are political regimes similar to that of Iraq.

US foreign policy fluctuates unexpectedly 'between euphoria and panic' (Kissinger). The US is an unreliable ally; it abandoned, for example, the Negus and the Shah. '. . . there have been political steps that have often muddled up our enemies with our friends. In our desire to be of help, we have instead put our foot in it and done a lot of harm' (Luttwak: 31). Although the US was in favour of European unity (preferably under its umbrella), it often perceives demonstrations of that unity as threats to its own objectives.

A European security policy is the unavoidable dimension of a European foreign policy. This implies that Europe pays for its own defence. The American criticism regarding the insufficient European share in Europe's defence is justified. Europe has the means to finance its defence. This does not exclude an alliance with the US. Finally, a situation must be avoided whereby non-European powers negotiate about Europe's future and whereby a Polignac or a Metternich could say again: 'On traitera de la paix chez vous, pour vous, sans vous'.

References

Cleveland, Harold van B. (1969), book review in *Columbia Journal of World Business*, September– October.

Johnson, Paul (1987), 'Europe: the sleeping princess', *European Affairs*, No. 1.

Luttwak, Edward N. (1988), in *La talpa nel labirinto*, 2 February.

Index

Note: Tables are shown in **bold** type.